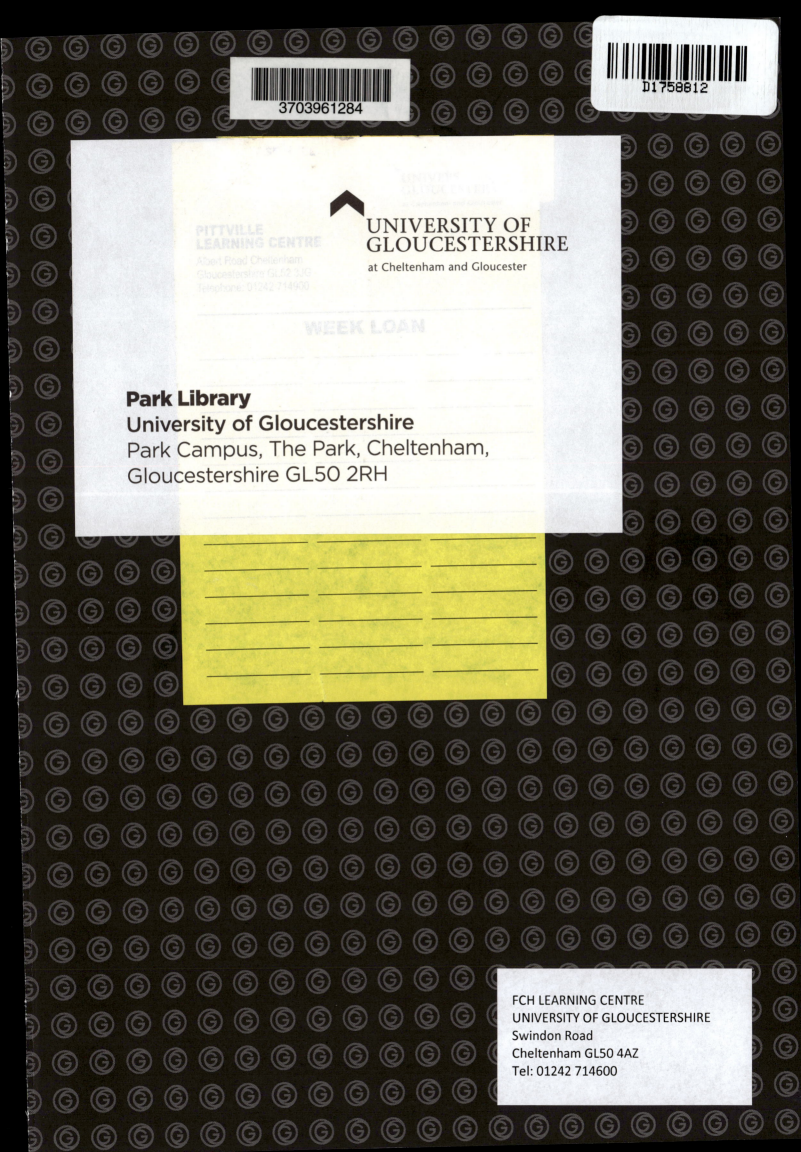

Published by **Graphis** | Publisher & Creative Director: B. Martin Pedersen | Design: Yon Joo Choi and Gregory Michael Cerrato | Editorial: Mark F. Bonner | Production: Ingrid Burrington | Webmaster: Kevin O'Neill | Sales & Marketing: Augusta Shifflett | Intern: Hyewon Shim

Remarks: We extend our heartfelt thanks to contributors throughout the world who have made it possible to publish a wide and international spectrum of the best work in this field. Entry instructions for all Graphis Books may be requested from: Graphis Inc., 307 Fifth Avenue, Tenth Floor, New York, New York 10016, or visit our web site at www.graphis.com.

Anmerkungen: Unser Dank gilt den Einsendern aus aller Welt, die es uns ermöglicht haben, ein breites, internationales Spektrum der besten Arbeiten zu veröffentlichen. Teilnahmebedingungen für die Graphis-Bücher sind erhältlich bei: Graphis, Inc., 307 Fifth Avenue, Tenth Floor, New York, New York 10016. Besuchen Sie uns im World Wide Web, www.graphis.com.

Remerciements: Nous remercions les participants du monde entier qui ont rendu possible la publication de cet ouvrage offrant un panorama complet des meilleurs travaux. Les modalités d'inscription peuvent être obtenues auprès de: Graphis, Inc., 307 Fifth Avenue, Tenth Floor, New York, New York 10016. Rendez-nous visite sur notre site web: www.graphis.com.

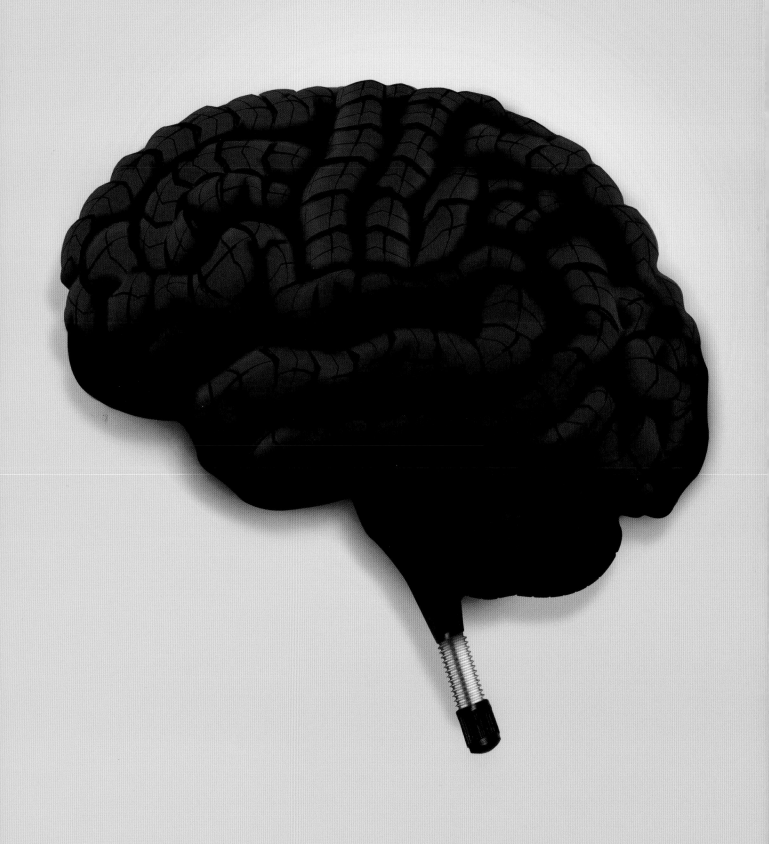

Contents

InMemoriam 6

Publisher'sLetter 9

Judges 10

GraphisNotedPhotographers 12

PlatinumWinners 30

WinnersByLocation 33

Automotive 34

AutoProducts 44

Beauty&Cosmetics 48

Beverages 50

Billboards/Outdoor 60

Broadcast/TV 74

Communications 82

Computers/Electronics 84

Education 90

Events 92

Fashion 100

Film 108

Food 110

Museums 122

Music 130

Products 134

ProfessionalServices 142

PublicService 162

Publishing 186

Restaurants 188

Retail 194

Self-Promotions 202

Sports 206

Tobacco 212

Travel 214

Websites 226

Zoos 232

Index 234

GraphisAdvertisements 238

InMemoriam

Edward Gelsthorpe
Consumer Products Marketer
1921-2009

Andrew Jaffe
Vice President, Adweek
1938-2010

Billy Mays
TV Pitchman
1959-2009

Charles Peebler
Chief Executive,
Bozell & Jacobs
1936-2009

Howard Zieff
Commercial Director &
Advertising Photographer
1927-2009

My congratulations to the Platinum and Gold winners in this first of our Graphis Annuals presenting the 100 Best.

In the future, entries not selected for the Top 100 will remain on our website and will automatically be considered for a Silver Award in our Advertising Journal, which will be accepting up to 1,000 winners.

As you can see in this book, each winning entry is given a full page on the spread along with complete credits and a description of the work with an explanation or case study of the assignment.

When each successive new Annual and Journal is introduced, the past year's work will automatically be entered into our archives. The archive will be an immediate inspirational tool that will present work through our search engine by subject, category, company or individuals — much faster than going to your bookshelf. We are also developing our Graphis past and present Masters section, selected from the consistent winners in our past books and annuals.

I still believe that our printed books will survive, however in much shorter print runs. When ordering our books in the future, you will receive the digital version immediately, with the physical book following in the mail. When the book is sold out, the digital copy will always be available.

There is much more in development, so please visit our website at *graphis.com*. Thank you for your continued support and inspiration.

B. Martin Pedersen
Graphis CEO & Creative Director

Dana Iraj Mirza Alikhani

Florian Metz

Saurabh Nayampalli

Doug Pedersen

Rich Silverstein

Omar Vulpinari

DANA IRAJ MIRZA ALIKHANI
Art Director, Ashna Advertising Agency
Iraj was born in Tehran, Iran. He received a BA in Visual Communication, Faculty of Fine Arts, at Tehran University, and was a Lecturer of Graphic Design at Tehran universities. He began his professional activities in graphic design in 1984, establishing Ashna Advertising Agency in 1991. He has been an agent and distributor of Graphis Inc. (Switzerland) in Iran, was a representative of IGDS in Icograda Regional Meeting, Istanbul in 2000, was an invited lecturer to the 13th National Youth Festival of Plastic Arts, and has been a lecturer at the Workshop of Graphic Design in Political Propaganda. Ashna Advertising Agency works in the fields of Design, Advertising, Mass Media (Billboards, TV, Radio), Marketing Research and Public Relations. It has managed to perform several major projects of PR and developed good relationships with printed media. Its international roster of clients includes Samsung of Korea, Toyota of Japan, Staedtler of Germany and Pepsi of Iran, among others. Ashna Advertising also does pro-bono publicity work for NGOs that include the Kahrizak Home for the Elderly and the Disabled (KHDS) and the MS Society of Iran.

FLORIAN METZ
Art Director, Heye, Group GmbH
Born in 1977 and raised in southern Germany, Florian Metz studied typographic design in Basel, Switzerland. During the last 10 years, he worked for different design and advertising agencies and as a freelance designer focused on typography and corporate design.
Florian Metz is now based in Munich working as an Art Director with Heye & Partner, an advertising agency for integrated brand communication that is member of the international agency network DDB Worldwide Communications Group. Heye has been one of Germany's most successful creative agencies for many years, and is among the 20 biggest agencies in the country by revenue. There, Florian has created advertising campaigns for international clients such as McDonald's, Sky Television, Elle and others, as well as Corporate Designs and social campaigns. His work was awarded both nationally and internationally and his projects have been published in renowned international publications.

SAURABH NAYAMPALLI
Associate Creative Director, Percept/H Pvt. Ltd.
Saurabh Nayampalli graduated from Raheja School of Applied Art (B.F.A.), Mumbai, India in 1999. In a career spanning eleven years, he has worked with agencies like Speer, Publicis Ambience and O&M. Currently, he is working as Associate Creative Director at Percept/H. Saurabh has worked with clients like Electrolux, Canon Cameras and Printers, Toyota Fortuner, Victorinox Swiss Army Knives, Fedex, Hero Honda, Pantaloons Retail, Bajaj Allianz Life Insurance, Bank of Baroda, MTNL Telecom, IndiaFirst Life Insurance, Nahar Builders, Sahara FILMY, Tata Safari, Tata Sumo, Amaron Batteries, SBI Life Insurance, Good Morning Tea, Star TV group of channels, Indian programming for DIRECTV and more. Awards Saurabh has won include Gold in Graphis Advertising Annual 2009 in Print Category for Pepperico Red Chilli Sauce; Silver World Medal in New York Festivals 2004 in Outdoor/Poster Category for Sil Chillivilli Red Chilli Sauce; finalist in ABBYs (Press Ad for Sil Chillivilli Red Chilli Sauce); and a Sil Chillivilli Red Chilli Sauce Poster was selected to be printed in the Showcase of Indian Advertising.

DOUG PEDERSEN
Associate Creative Director/Art Director, Carmichael Lynch
Doug is a graduate of the University of Texas in Austin. Though he loved Texas, he hated the heat and left in search of cooler climates. Thus he spent 9 years in Charlotte, NC at the highly-awarded Loeffler Ketchum Mountjoy. After that, it was on to Crispin Porter + Bogusky in Miami and Carmichael Lynch in Minneapolis (where he currently works). Over the course of his 12+ years in advertising, Doug has had the fortune to produce advertising campaigns for Volkswagen, Harley-Davidson, Subaru, Outward Bound, Schutt Sports, Redfeather Snowshoes, Burger King, Miller Lite, North Carolina Tourism and a long list of others.
Though advertising keeps him pretty busy, Doug still finds time to take in more than his fair share of movies and music and occasionally dabbles in creating his own art.

RICH SILVERSTEIN
Co-Chairman & Creative Director, Goodby, Silverstein & Partners
Rich grew up in Yorktown Heights, New York. After graduating from the Parsons School of Design in New York City, he moved to San Francisco against his father's wishes, sure that he would be back in three months. He worked as an art director for Rolling Stone magazine and five different advertising agencies before founding his own company in 1984 with Jeff Goodby.
Goodby, Silverstein & Partners has been awarded Agency of the Year from various organizations 23 times, and in 2009 they were honored as Digital Agency of the Year at the Cannes advertising festival. AdWeek has named the company Agency of the Decade, and named Rich and Jeff Executives of the Decade. In 2002 he was inducted into the New York Art Directors Club Hall of Fame, and two years later into The One Club Creative Hall of Fame.
Rich is equally passionate about projects away from work, from creating his own art to visually blogging for The Huffington Post. He's helped to make the Golden Gate National Parks Conservancy a brand that is the envy of America's park system. He serves on the board of Specialized Bicycles and the United States Cycling Federation's development committee.
Rich lives in Mill Valley, California with his wife Carla Emil and his cat Felix, and considers himself to be extremely lucky to be able to ride his bike over the Golden Gate Bridge to and from work each day.

OMAR VULPINARI
Creative Director & Head of Visual Communication, Fabrica
Omar Vulpinari was born in the Republic of San Marino and raised in the United States. Today he lives in Treviso, Italy.
Since 1998, Vulpinari has been Head of Visual Communication at Fabrica, the Benetton communications center founded by Luciano Benetton and Oliviero Toscani. Here, he has been creative director for advertising and communication design projects for United Nations, Lawyers Committee for Human Rights, Witness, Amnesty International, Without Borders, Instituto Terra, United Colors of Benetton, ArteFiera Bologna, Istituto Luce, Porsche, Vespa, The New Yorker Magazine, Walrus Magazine, Design Issues – MIT Press, Domus Magazine, Corriere della Sera, La Repubblica, Electa, Mondadori, and Cult TV – Fox International.
Fabrica's visual communication work under his direction has been featured by major international media and dedicated exhibitions at the GGG in Tokyo, the DDD in Osaka, and the ZeroOne Design Center in Seoul. In the exhibition "Fabrica: Les Yeux Ouverts" it was featured at the Centre Pompidou in Paris, La Triennale di Milano and the Shanghai Art Museum. Fabrica was the recent winner of the Graphis Platinum Advertising Award for the UNWHO Child Safety print campaign. Vulpinari is also responsible the center's transdisciplinary workshop program Environmental, Social, Relational.
Vulpinari has been a frequent speaker and juror for major international design events organized by ICOGRADA, AGI, AIGA, ISTD, JAGDA, Profile Intermedia, GraficEurope, and numerous others. He is an advisor for United Nations World Health Organization and Design 21 – Social Design Network. He is also Regional Ambassador for INDEX: Design to Improve Life Awards. He teaches Communication Design at the IUAV University of Venice. Omar is currently vice president of ICOGRADA – International Council of Graphic Design Associations.

GraphisNotedPhotographers

joSon www.josonphoto.com

Parish Kohanim www.parishkohanim.com

John Madere www.johnmadere.com

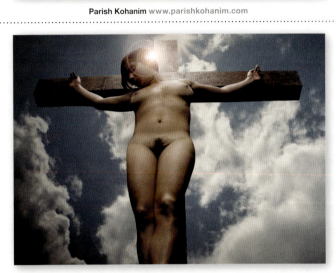

Phil Marco www.philmarco.com

R.J. Muna www.rjmuna.com

Lennette Newell www.lennettenewell.com

Francois Robert www.francoisrobertphotography.com

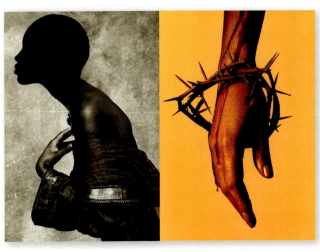

Albert Watson www.albertwatson.com

Naomi Campbell, Palm Springs, 1989
Omahyra, Hand with Thorns, New York City, 2004

“Francois transcends language and ideology. His work, both artistic and commercial, is unsurpassed among photographers today.” Massimo Vignelli, New York

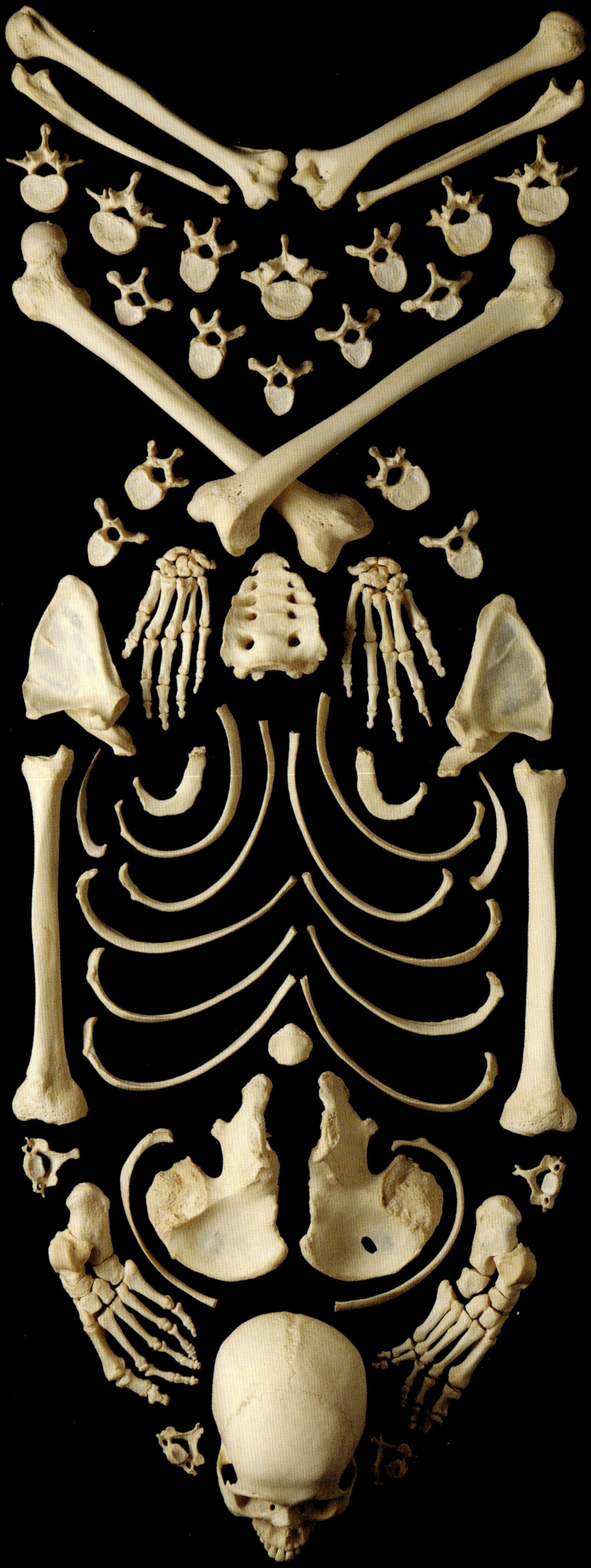

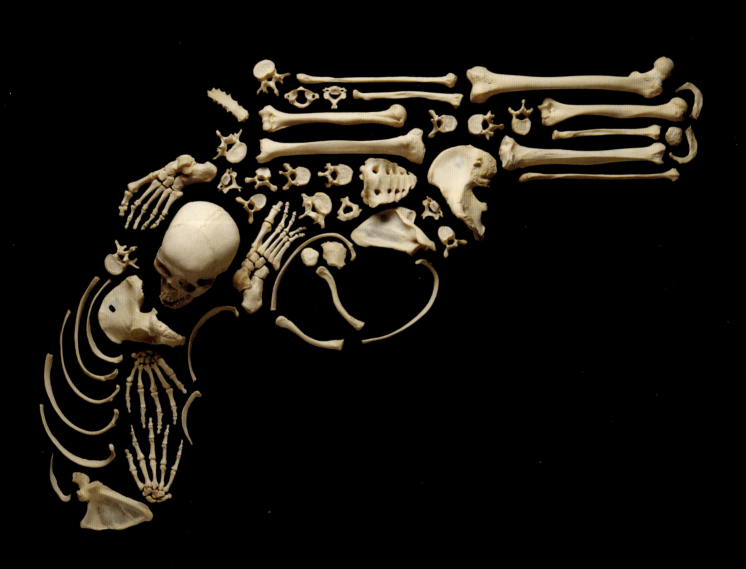

Lennette Newell
photography

www.lennettenewell.com   1-877-930-9229

RJ MUNA

STUDIO 415.285.8300

REPRESENTED BY
MARIANNE CAMPBELL ASSOCIATES
415.433.0353

PHILMARCO

www.philmarco.com

JOHNMADERE.COM

303 PARK AVENUE SOUTH
NEW YORK, NY 10010
212-966-4136

JOHN MADERE PHOTOGRAPHY

childhood : pets

joSon photo studio   415 252 0291   joSonphoto.com

Pyper Paul + Kenney, Tampa, FL, USA | www.pyperpaul.com / Client: Tires Plus / Title: Tires Plus Anatomy
Campaign: Brake Disc Eye, Tire Brain, Engine Heart / Account Directors: Jesse Vahsholtz, Garrett Garcia
/ Art Director: Kris Gregoire / Associate Creative Director: Michael Schillig / Copywriter: Michael Schillig
/ Executive Creative Director: Tom Kenney / P. 46

O'Leary & Partners, Newport Beach, CA, USA | www.adagency.com / Client: Mothers Polishes / Title:
Deep Shine: Coins, Leaf, Bobber / Art Director: Eric Spiegler / Executive Creative Directors: Eric Spiegler,
Deidre McQuaide / Print Producer: Carol Knaeps / P. 44

Publicis Dallas, USA | www.publicis-usa.com / Client: Terminix / Title: Sawdust House / Agency Producer:
Jaime Roderer / Art Director: Dustin Taylor / Copywriter: Andrew Beckman / Creative Directors: Julia
Melle, Pete Voehringer, Steve Grimes / Executive Creative Director: Shon Rathbone / Photographer: Scott
Harben / P. 146

JWT Chile, Santiago, Chile | www.jwt.com / Client: Scrabble / Title: Scrabble / Art Director: Matias Lecaros
/ Creative Directors: Matías Lecaros, Sergio Rosati / Copywriter: Matías Lecaros / Executive Creative
Director: Leo Farfan / Illustrator: Boris Berstel / Photographer: Cristián Gastello / P. 140

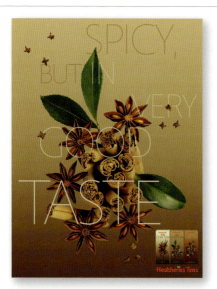

Shine, Auckland, New Zealand | www.shinelimited.co.nz / Client: Heal-
theries / Title: Healtheries Print - Spicy, Bloom, Boiling / Art Director:
Len Cheeseman / Creative Director: Lucien Law / Designers: Emile
Holmewood, Stephen Cicala / P. 50

Goodby, Silverstein & Partners, San Francisco, USA | www.goodbysil-
verstein.com / Client: Quaker / Title: Quaker Magazine / Art Director: Cris Logan / Creative Directors: Jamie Barrett, Will McGinness
/ Copywriter: Jamie Barrett / P. 110

MacLaren McCann Calgary, Canada | www.maclaren.com / Client:
Randell's Drycleaning / Title: Nature's Favourite Drycleaner / Art Di-
rectors: Mike Meadus, Natalie Santucci / Associate Creative Director:
Nicolle Pittman / Creative Director: Mike Meadus / Photographer:
Justen Lacoursiere / Copywriter: Nicolle Pittman / P. 142

1907

1917

1927

1937

Buy eye-glasses before it's too late.

TBWA\PHS Helsinki, Finland | **www.tbwa.fi** / Client: Instrumentarium / Title: Picasso, Matisse / Account Director: Eija Anteroinen / Art Directors: Mikko Torvinen, Ossi Honkanen / Copywriters: Erkko Mannila, Tommy Makinen, Antti Toivonen / Creative Director: Mikko Torvinen / Illustrator: Tommi Vallisto / Project Managers: Karolina Mattsson, Kirsi Parni / **P. 198**

I know we were doing your taxes, but since those files don't exist anymore I have a
better idea. Don't do your taxes. Seriously, just don't do them.

WHAT'S_THE_WORST_THAT_CAN_HAPPEN?

Sure the feds might come after you and charge you for tax evasion. But not if you have
a plan. Here's what you're going to do. You're going to pack a suitcase with enough
clothes for a week. Then you're going to wake up tomorrow just like any other day, kiss
your wife and kids goodbye and go to work. Then you're going to drive right past the
office, head south and don't stop driving until you're in Mexico.

Think about it. It's just you, the open road and your fake beard blowing in the wind.
When you arrive your new name is Juan Pablo Ramirez and your father died in the war.
If they ask which war, throw them off by listing Taco Bell menu items and then
run away like, well, like you're a fugitive from justice, which you are.

Live as a drifter in Mexico

*** until your family assumes you're dead and more importantly until good old Revenue
Canada assumes you're dead. Then you can return to your old life, explain to your
children daddy was working over-overtime and they should call you Juan now, and you'll
never pay taxes again.

GET_YOUR_FILES_BACK. CALL_PC_MEDICS_AT_403_606_7234

TAXI CANADA INC, Calgary, Canada | **www.taxi.ca** / Client: PC Medic / Title: PC Medic Blue Screen of Death Campaign / Account Director: Ginny Wetmore / Art Director: Kelsey Horne / Creative Director: Trent Burton / Print Producer: Marsha Walters / Copywriter: Nick Asik / **P. 84**

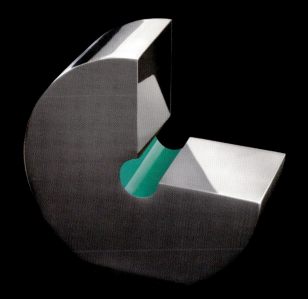

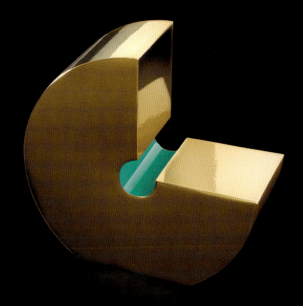

THE AMERICAS

North America:
Canada 013
United States 075
Greenland 000

Caribbean:
Anguilla 000
Antigua and Barbuda 000
Aruba 000
Bahamas 000
Barbados 000
Bermuda 000
British Virgin Islands 000
Cayman Islands 000
Cuba 000
Dominica 000
Dominican Republic 000
Grenada 000
Guadeloupe 000
Haiti 000
Jamaica 000
Martinique 000
Montserrat 000
Netherlands Antilles 000
Puerto Rico 000
Saint Kitts and Nevis 000
Saint Lucia 000
Saint Vincent & the Grenadines .. 000
Trinidad and Tobago 000
Turks & Caicos Islands 000
U.S. Virgin Islands 000

Central America:
Belize 000
Costa Rica 000
El Salvador 000
Guatemala 000
Honduras 000
Mexico 000
Nicaragua 000
Panama 000

South America:
Argentina 000
Bolivia 000
Brazil 000
Chile 001
Colombia 000
Ecuador 000
Falkland Islands (Malvinas) 000
French Guiana 000
Guyana 000
Paraguay 000
Peru 000
Suriname 000
Uruguay 000
Venezuela 000

EUROPE & AFRICA

Eastern Europe:
Belarus 000
Bulgaria 000
Czech Republic 000
Hungary 000
Poland 000
Republic of Moldova 000
Romania 000
Russian Federation 000
Slovakia 000
Ukraine 000

Northern Europe:
Channel Islands 000
Denmark 000
Estonia 000
Faeroe Islands 000
Finland 002
Iceland 000
Ireland 000
Isle of Man 000
Latvia 000
Lithuania 000
Norway 000
Sweden 000
United Kingdom 001

Southern Europe:
Albania 000
Andorra 000
Bosnia and Herzegovina 000
Croatia 001
Gibraltar 000
Greece 000
Holy See 000
Italy 000
Macedonia 000
Malta 000
Montenegro 000
Portugal 000
San Marino 000
Serbia 000
Slovenia 000
Spain 001

Western Europe:
Austria 000
Belgium 001
France 000
Germany 000
Liechtenstein 000
Luxembourg 000
Monaco 000
Netherlands 000
Switzerland 000

Eastern Africa:
Burundi 000
Comoros 000
Djibouti 000
Eritrea 000
Ethiopia 000
Kenya 000
Madagascar 000
Malawi 000
Mauritius 000
Mayotte 000
Mozambique 000
Réunion 000
Rwanda 000
Seychelles 000
Somalia 000
Uganda 000
United Republic of Tanzania 000
Zambia 000
Zimbabwe 000

Middle Africa:
Angola 000
Cameroon 000
Central African Republic 000
Chad 000
Republic of the Congo 000
Equatorial Guinea 000
Gabon 000
São Tomé and Principe 000

Northern Africa:
Algeria 000
Egypt 000
Libya 000
Morocco 000
Sudan 000
Tunisia 000
Western Sahara 000

Southern Africa:
Botswana 000
Lesotho 000

Namibia 000
South Africa 000
Swaziland 000

Western Africa:
Benin 000
Burkina Faso 000
Cape Verde 000
Côte d'Ivoire 000
Gambia 000
Ghana 000
Guinea 000
Guinea-Bissau 000
Liberia 000
Mali 000
Mauritania 000
Niger 000
Saint Helena 000
Senegal 000
Sierra Leone 000
Togo 000

ASIA & OCEANIA

Eastern Asia:
China 000
Democratic People's Republic of Korea 000
Japan 001
Mongolia 000
Republic of Korea 000

South-central Asia:
Afghanistan 000
Bangladesh 000
Bhutan 000
India 000
Iran 000
Kazakhstan 000
Kyrgyzstan 000
Maldives 000
Nepal 000
Pakistan 000
Sri Lanka 000
Tajikistan 000
Turkmenistan 000
Uzbekistan 000

South-eastern Asia:
Brunei Darussalam 000
Cambodia 000
Indonesia 000
Lao People's Democratic Republic 000
Malaysia 000
Myanmar 000
Philippines 000
Singapore 000
Thailand 000
Timor-Leste 000

Western Asia:
Vietnam 000
Armenia 000
Azerbaijan 000
Bahrain 000
Cyprus 000
Georgia 000
Iraq 000
Israel 000
Jordan 000
Kuwait 000
Lebanon 000
Oman 000
Palestine 000
Qatar 000
Saudi Arabia 000
Syrian Arab Republic 000
Turkey 000
United Arab Emirates 001
Yemen 000

Melanesia:
Fiji 000
New Caledonia 000
Papua New Guinea 000
Solomon Islands 000
Vanuatu 000

Micronesia:
Guam 000
Kiribati 000
Marshall Islands 000
Federated States of Micronesia ..000
Nauru 000
Northern Mariana Islands 000
Palau 000

Polynesia:
American Samoa 000
Cook Islands 000
French Polynesia 000
Niue 000
Pitcairn 000
Samoa 000
Tokelau 000
Tonga 000
Tuvalu 000
Wallis and Futuna Islands 000
Australia 002
New Zealand 001

TOTAL WINNING ENTRIES **100**

Opposite page: Award photograph by Henry Leutwyler

Ad Agency: STIR, Milwaukee, WI, USA | www.stirstuff.com   **Client:** Urban Motorworx   **Title:** Cleanerschlagens   **Account Director:** Brian Bennett

Art Director: Matt Johanning   **Associate Creative Director:** Scott Shalles   **Copywriter:** Scott Shalles

Creative Director: Bill Kresse   **Designer:** Sara Neuman   **Digital Artist/Multimedia:** Brian Steenstry

ASSIGNMENT

Introduce Urban Motorworx to BMW automobile owners as an alternative to more expensive dealership service without sacrificing expertise. Urban Motorworx is a highly specialized BMW service center with factory-trained BMW Technicians.

APPROACH

In these times more than ever, people are conscious of their expenses. And, when it comes to servicing an expensive German import, it can get rather costly at a dealership. We set out to capture the attention of BMW owners and inform them that they have an alternative to expensive dealership service. With Urban Motorworx they can get the same expertise of service the dealership offers without having to get a second mortgage.

THE BIG IDEA

While concepting we came up with headlines that ended with a humorous twist on the German language. This twist gave the brand a tonality that allowed us to tout Urban Motorworx's affordability in a whimsical, less-chest-beating way. The lines were just fun to read so we made them the focal point. We also used the iconic BMW front grill and swapped out the BMW logo with the Urban Motorworx logo to emphasize that they work exclusively on BMW automobiles. There's minimal body copy that gets straight to the point about Urban Motorworx's affordability.

RESULTS

Urban Motorworx loved the work. After the campaign was introduced, Urban Motorworx experienced about a 30% increase in new customers.

FOR AN
AUTHENTIC
DEALERSHIP EXPERIENCE

◆

WE'LL MAKE YOU WAIT A WEEK
AND THEN TAKE YOU TO THE

Cleanerschlagens.

Urban MotorworX

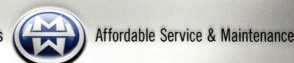

Factory-trained BMW Technicians   Affordable Service & Maintenance

urbanmotorworx.com

Ad Agency: Goodby, Silverstein & Partners, San Francisco, USA | www.gspsf.com   **Client:** Hyundai   **Title:** Genesis Coupe Launch Print

Art Director: Chris Toland   **Creative Director:** Jeff Goodby   **Copywriter:** Jim Elliott

When you're Hyundai, just trying to convince the world that you've built a competitive four-door sedan is an uphill battle. Now imagine trying to launch the first race-worthy sports coupe in your company's history. In the spring of 2009, this was the uphill battle Hyundai was facing with the launch of the Genesis Coupe — a shock to the category loaded with everything enthusiasts dream about. We needed to let the Coupe's genuine performance capabilities speak for themselves. As part of a larger integrated effort, this consumer print campaign placed a race car driver's mentality boldly on the open road.

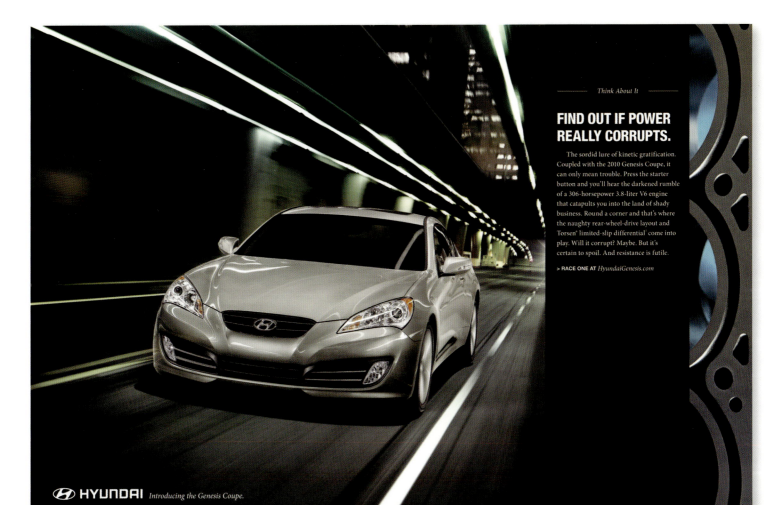

———— *Think About It* ————

FIND OUT IF POWER REALLY CORRUPTS.

The sordid lure of kinetic gratification. Coupled with the 2010 Genesis Coupe, it can only mean trouble. Press the starter button and you'll hear the darkened rumble of a 306-horsepower 3.8-liter V6 engine that catapults you into the land of shady business. Round a corner and that's where the naughty rear-wheel-drive layout and Torsen® limited-slip differential¹ come into play. Will it corrupt? Maybe. But it's certain to spoil. And resistance is futile.

> RACE ONE AT *HyundaiGenesis.com*

⟨H⟩ HYUNDAI *Introducing the Genesis Coupe.*

———— *Think About It* ————

G-FORCE BEATS WRINKLE CREAM.

Youth in a tube? Spare us. What you really need are the rejuvenating properties of the all-new 2010 Genesis Coupe. Namely, a 306-horsepower 3.8-liter V6 engine that will stretch your face into an adolescent grimace and a rear-wheel-drive powertrain that will have you giggling like a child around the bends. As for the Brembo® braking system? That's for keeping the new you from running completely amok. Careful, now. This is powerful stuff.

> RACE ONE AT *HyundaiGenesis.com*

⟨H⟩ HYUNDAI *Introducing the Genesis Coupe.*

Ad Agency: Lewis Communications, Birmingham, AL, USA | www.lewiscommunications.com   **Client:** Tiffin Motorhomes   **Title:** Tiffin 2010 Ad Campaign

Account Directors: Val Holman, Beth Bailey, Sarah Hardekopf   **Art Director:** Spencer Till

Copywriter: Spencer Till   **Creative Director:** Stephen Curry   **Executive Creative Director:** Spencer Till

Photographer: Jeff Williams   **Photographer's Assistant:** Benjamin Fine   **Print Producers:** Benjamin Fine, Leigh Ann Motley

One can hardly think of a more challenging set of circumstances. A nationwide economic collapse. Plummeting home values. And an RV industry that was on the verge of disappearing. To make matters worse, strict bank underwriting was making RV loans virtually impossible to come by. Yet our client, Tiffin, had several advantages. A strong financial position, a fiercely loyal customer base, and a longstanding reputation for standing behind their products in good times and bad. Our campaign sought to do two things. First, we needed to give people a dose of perspective.

Our goal was to help people take the long view — that even during an economic recession, there are precious family moments that can never again be recaptured. If anything, time is more precious than ever. And with a substantial media buy, we wanted to reinforce the image of Tiffin as one of the survivors — a company that emerged from the economic morass stronger than ever, and ready to support their products for years to come. Today, the Tiffin plant is operating at full capacity, and dealers can't get enough of their product.

Ad Agency: Cramer Krasselt, Milwaukee, WI, USA | www.c-k.com   **Client:** Can-Am Spyder Roadster   **Title:** Need The Most, What Is It?

Art Directors: Shawn Holpfer, Brian Steinseifer   **Copywriters:** Brian Chin, Chris Jacobs

Creative Director: Todd Stone   **Executive Creative Director:** Chris Jacobs   **Photographer:** Jeff Salzer

When you have a vehicle as unexpected as the three-wheeled Can-Am Spyder Roadster, you pretty much want it to be the star of the advertising. So that's exactly what we did. We chose angles and croppings of the Spyder that best displayed its unique design. This machine is impossible to ignore when you see one on the road. And we wanted to make it equally impossible to ignore on the printed page.

From there we married the designs with headlines that we knew would resonate with our target market. The line "Man I love it. What is it?" not only introduced the Spyder to the world, but touched on the fact that this machine is so magnetic, people fall in love with it before they even know what it is. After all, this isn't just a new vehicle. It's a new category of vehicle.

Our second execution was created specifically for the Robb Report. This is an audience that basically collects expensive toys. And we wanted Spyder to make it to the top of their toy wish list. Thus, the headline, "Of all the things you don't need, this is the one you need the most." The reviewers at Adweek perhaps put it best when they said: "The ad's mixture of brashness and realism wouldn't work for every product, but it seems in sync with the self-image of the people most likely to buy these things." That was kind of our goal, really. To talk to our audience in a relevant way — and create advertising as unique as the product itself.

"MAN, I LOVE IT. WHAT IS IT?"

Meet the Can-Am™ Spyder® roadster. Its sequential electronic 5-speed transmission (SE5) puts a powerful Rotax® 990 V-Twin engine at your command. Dynamic Power Steering (DPS™) and a Vehicle Stability System (VSS) help refine your ride. And its unique, three-wheeled configuration ensures no head will be left unturned. Learn more at spyder.brp.com.

Ad Agency: The Brandon Agency, Myrtle Beach, FL, USA | www.thebrandonagency.com   **Client:** Best Golf Cars   **Title:** GPS, Immature Adults

Art Director: Jon Leon   **Artist:** Hacjob   **Copywriter:** James Rosene   **Photographer:** Matt Silk

Based on insight garnered through research, Best Golf Cars asked The Brandon Agency to create a campaign that revealed how people are using golf cars as a social tool — such as cruising the neighborhood, stopping to chat with neighbors, enjoying cocktails and most importantly, making a status statement based on the amount of customization. The campaign featured posters and print ads.

ROOM FOR 2 ADULTS AND 2 KIDS.
OR 2 ADULTS AND 2 REALLY
IMMATURE ADULTS.

Club Car

Ad Agency: O'Leary & Partners, Newport Beach, CA, USA | www.adagency.com   **Client:** Mothers Polishes   **Title:** Deep Shine: Coins, Leaf, Bobber

Art Director: Eric Spiegler   **Executive Creative Directors:** Eric Spiegler, Deidre McQuaide   **Print Producer:** Carol Knaeps

We were asked to develop a campaign for the Mothers FX line of waxes and polishes. These products use the most advanced technology and formulas to provide the richest and deepest shine for today's automotive finishes. A deep, liquid, wet-looking shine as many car enthusiasts would put it. And we needed to visually demonstrate this shine in the executions.

This was one of those ideas where the execution could literally make or break it. Without a budget for a photo shoot, we worked closely with the guys at Mothers to find the ideal car shots. This was a bit of a challenge because we needed to find just the right angle in order to pull off the watery surface effect. But beyond that, the car had to have the right look. The Mothers guys are true car enthusiasts, and just any car, regardless of the angle or how nice the paint looks, just wouldn't suffice. Once we found the shots, we worked closely with our digital artist, Charlie Haygood of Bonus Arts, who helped us achieve the effect we were going for to perfection.

The overall goal was to communicate that Mothers FX products produces a brilliant, deep-looking shine – a shine so deep. Our ultimate solution was to literally turn the paint into water, by showing objects interacting with it. We explored all sorts of different visual cues — from shark fins to periscopes to straws — until finally settling on the fishing bobber, leaf and coins. We felt those objects told the story in a simple, subtle yet striking way.

Mothers was thrilled with the initial results and have since requested to have these ads produced into posters for retail stores, loyal customers and their corporate office. Visits to the Mothers site soared when the campaign broke, and the company enjoyed a healthy increase in sales.

Ad Agency: Pyper Paul + Kenney, Tampa, FL, USA | www.pyperpaul.com   **Client:** Tires Plus   **Title:** Tires Plus Anatomy Campaign: Brake Disc Eye, Tire Brain, Engine Heart

Account Directors: Jesse Vahsholtz, Garrett Garcia   **Art Director:** Kris Gregoire

Associate Creative Director: Michael Schillig   **Copywriter:** Michael Schillig   **Executive Creative Director:** Tom Kenney

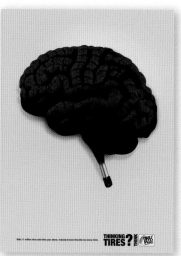

ASSIGNMENT

The assignment was to create an awareness campaign for Tires Plus that would educate consumers on their long-standing brand heritage, proven experience and diverse capabilities within the car care industry.

APPROACH

The challenge was to concept and execute a truly unique campaign that would cut through the huge amount of screaming, price-driven advertising in this category. We wanted to instantly capture consumers' attention by positioning Tires Plus as a car care expert, yet still maintain a highly personalized human quality within the ads.

THE BIG IDEA

Our solution was this fittingly named "Anatomy" campaign. We developed three different ads, each focusing on a different human body part (brain, heart and eye) which were created out of tires or car parts. We then used each of these prominent body parts to visually convey a main benefit of Tires Plus.

RESULTS

Through these ads, we were able to bring Tires Plus's greatest benefits to life in a very distinctive way that has helped them generate a tremendous amount of buzz in a highly competitive market.

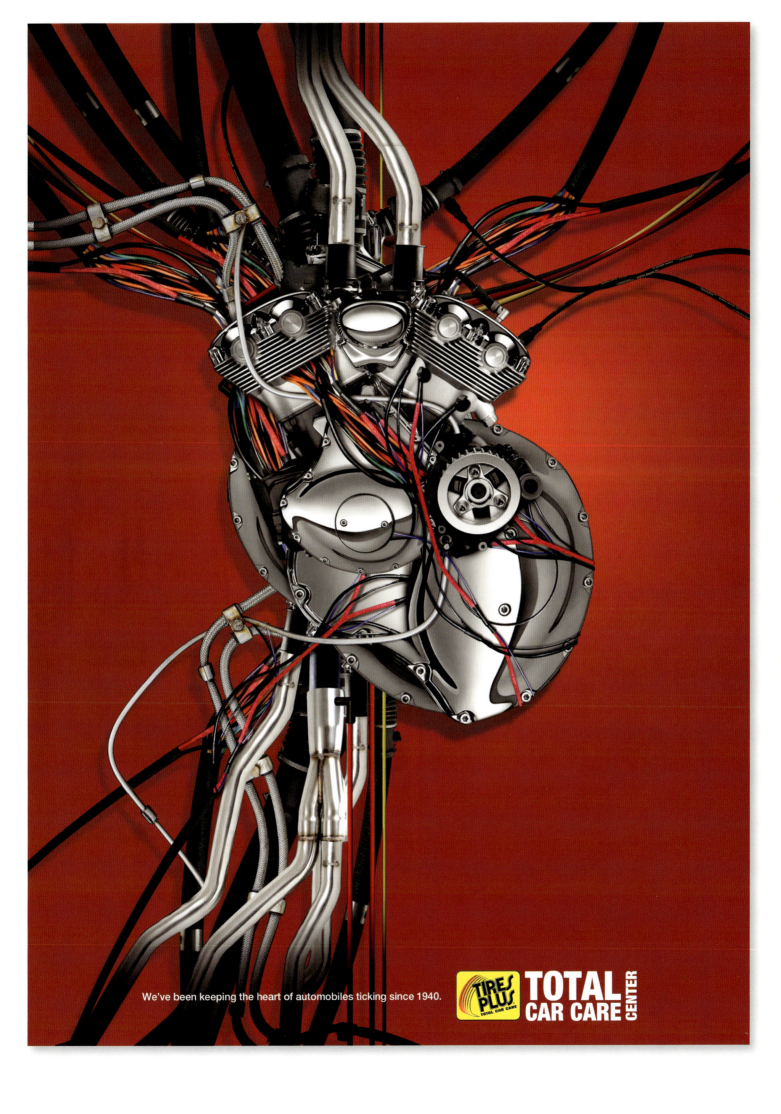

We've been keeping the heart of automobiles ticking since 1940.

TIRES PLUS
TOTAL CAR CARE

TOTAL
CAR CARE CENTER

Ad Agency: MacLaren McCann Calgary, Canada | www. maclaren.com   **Client:** Smoothe Laser Clinics   **Title:** Unnaturally Smooth

Art Director: Sean Mitchell   **Creative Director:** Mike Meadus   **Photographer:** Noah Fallis   **Copywriter:** Sean Mitchell

Based on the conclusion that there's nothing natural about being perfectly hairless, this somewhat risqué idea delivers some sensationally subtle ideas about laser hair removal.

By leveraging the viewer's realization that this isn't a real woman, the ad shows how Smoothe can take women to an unnatural state of sexy perfection—and become the flawless doll they've always dreamed of being. Through a number of media channels, the campaign turned Smoothe from another generic option into the hot new spot for women to get perfect skin.

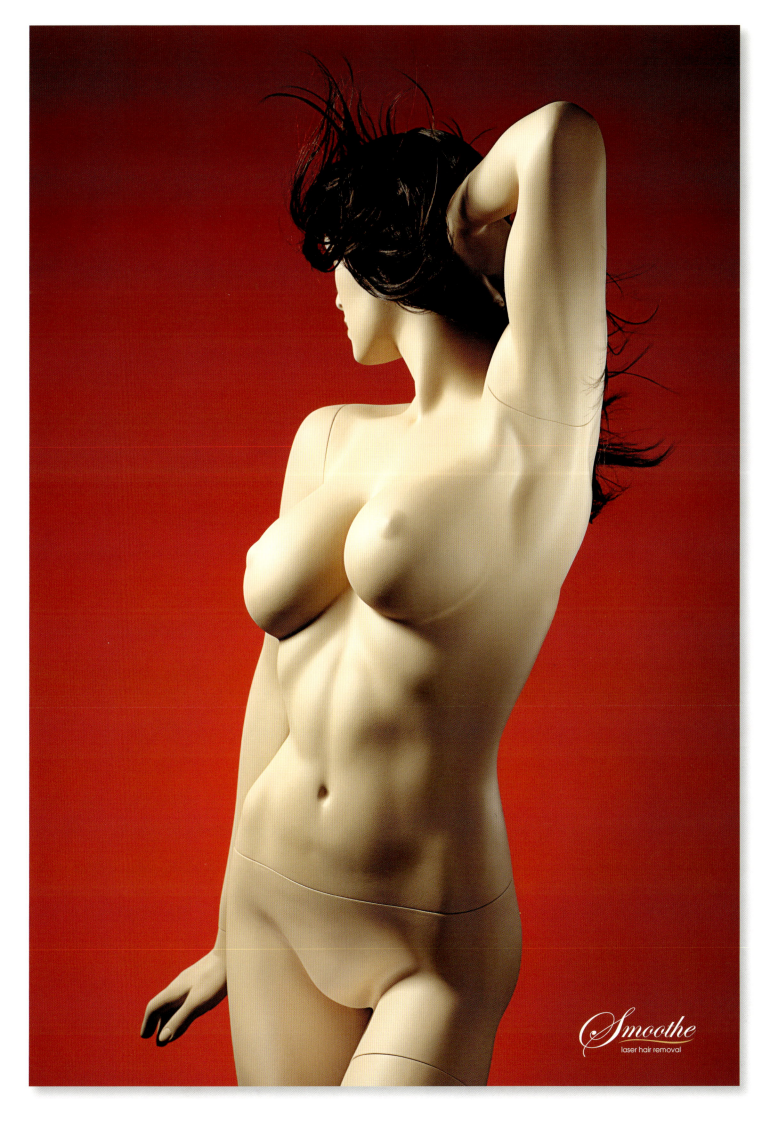

Smoothe
laser hair removal

Ad Agency: Shine, Auckland, New Zealand | www.shinelimited.co.nz   **Client:** Healtheries   **Title:** Healtheries Print - Spicy, Bloom, Boiling

Art Director: Len Cheeseman   **Creative Director:** Lucien Law   **Designers:** Emile Holmewood, Stephen Cicala

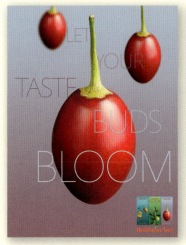 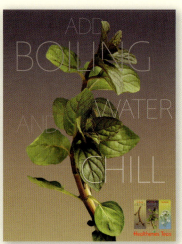

ASSIGNMENT

Healtheries was the first brand in green and herbal tea in New Zealand. The new packaging design for Healtheries tea was designed to re-establish Healtheries leadership in the green and herbal tea category by injecting a sense of modernity, style and pleasure to the range. The aim of the other elements of the campaign was simply to showcase the new design.

APPROACH

As non-black teas have become more mainstream and new competitors entered the market, Healtheries was getting lost amongst the clutter. As well as reinforcing health credentials, the new design needed to inject a sense of modernity, style and pleasure to the range overall. We needed a design that created a strong family feel but also allowed different parts of the range — green, chai and fruit and herbal teas — to have their own specific identities.

THE BIG IDEA

We elected to keep it very simple by bringing to life the key elements of the design — exquisite photography of key ingredients and the Fedra Display typeface — and using these to reinforce the sensual pleasure of drinking a cup of Healtheries tea.

RESULTS

The redesign was integral to the re-launch of the "face of Healtheries." The Healtheries Tea portfolio has recently achieved five solid months of share gains (first time in three years), and is in great shape to carry on this growth given the next round of innovative Kiwi-themed products showcased in the new design.

Ad Agency: BCF, Virginia Beach, VA, USA | www.boomyourbrand.com | **Client:** Massimo Zanetti Beverage | **Title:** Heavenly | **Account Director:** Scott Schindele

Agency Producer: Brian Bobinski | **Art Director:** Keith Ireland | **Copywriter:** Kevin McCarthy | **Creative Director:** Keith Ireland | **Project Manager:** Laura Bolt

Since 1932, Chock full O'Nut's Heavenly Coffee jingle, along with the bright yellow and black packaging, has been a staple in New York City culture.

We wanted to capture that spirit with a campaign that embraced Chock full O'Nuts as a bold, no-nonsense coffee for the City That Never Sleeps. By incorporating the Heavenly messaging from the classic jingle, we were able to tug at the nostalgic heartstrings of modern New Yorkers and reinforce Chock as New York's coffee. Also, by showcasing the can as the main element of the ads, and using the yellow lid as the visual payoff, our audience could easily identify the Chock brand on their grocery store shelves.

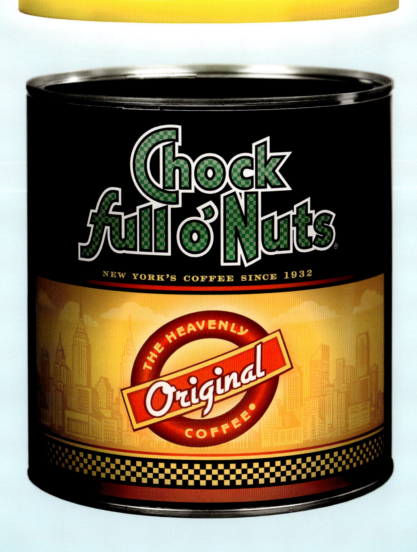

heavenly.™

Ad Agency: MacLaren McCann Calgary, Canada | www.maclaren.com   **Client:** CommuniTea Cafe   **Title:** Music Note

Art Directors: Mike Meadus, Mark Lovely   **Associate Creative Director:** Nicolle Pittman

Creative Director: Mike Meadus   **Photographer:** Justen Lacoursiere   **Copywriter:** Nicolle Pittman

Hidden in a Rocky Mountain valley, the Communitea Café in Canmore is a calm oasis surrounded by ridiculous peacefulness. Oversized beanbag chairs sit like marshmallows on the floor filled with sprawling Patagonia-types, beams of sunlight illuminating their noodle bowls.

Communitea's transition to late-night indie music venue needed to hint at this other side. We turned normal sights at the tea house (in this case a tea bag) into symbols of music (in this case a music note).

Communitea has since used the images for outside media with great results, as the feeling of the poster is so similar to the feeling of the café itself.

Their evening shows are typically sold out. Though we suspect there's a lot of people from lunch that never got around to leaving.

Live music every week.

Ad Agency: Ogilvy & Mather, New York, USA | www.ogilvy.com   **Client:** Coca-Cola/Hopenhagen   **Title:** A Bottle of Hope: Plant, Water, Recycling

Art Director: Justin Walsh   **Associate Creative Director:** Greg Gerstner   **Chief Creative Officer:** Tham Khai Meng

Executive Creative Directors: Greg Ketchum, Tom Godici   **Illustrator:** Andrew Bannecker   **Print Producers:** Rachel Fuller, Michael Piscatelli

ASSIGNMENT

On December 7, 2009, leaders from 192 countries met at the UN Climate Change Conference (COP15) in Copenhagen. During the months leading up to COP15, our assignment was to raise awareness for the conference while emphasizing the leadership role businesses must take to create a more sustainable planet.

CHALLENGES & APPROACH

Months before COP15 even started, the consensus was that an international treaty would not be signed. We decided early on that we wouldn't let the negativity surrounding the conference come through in our campaign. Instead, our approach was to develop a positive message of change that could connect every person, every city, every corporation and every nation to the city of Copenhagen. And eventually, help turn Copenhagen into Hopenhagen.

THE BIG IDEA

The Hopenhagen campaign became a movement, a moment and a chance at a new beginning. It was the hope that we can create a global community that will lead our leaders into making the right decisions. And the promise that if we all do our part to help solve the climate crisis, we could end up solving the economic crisis as well. Working in collaboration with illustrator Andrew Bannecker, we created the "Bottle of Hope" campaign around three of Coke's most accomplished sustainability initiatives — recycling, water conservation and the Plant Bottle made from up to 30% renewable plant-based materials. This campaign was featured predominately in Copenhagen during the conference and helped establish a positive outlook amongst the chaos of the talks.

RESULTS

With the "Bottle of Hope" campaign, Coke significantly extended the reach of the Hopenhagen movement among opinion leaders and environmentally aware consumers — and helped create a vital new community of nearly 6 million passionate and empowered citizens of Hopenhagen. These citizens are already using their collective power to make sure that the COP PlantBottlemade 16 conference brings us even closer to a ratified treaty and a more sustainable way of life.

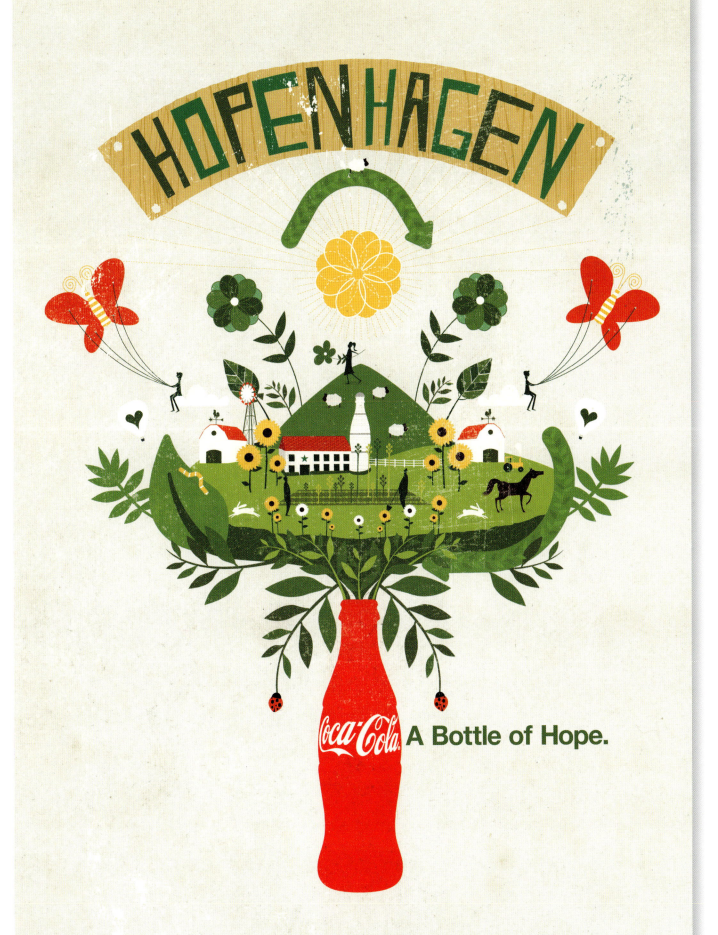

Ad Agency: DeVito/Verdi, New York, USA | www.devitoverdi.com   **Client:** Appleton Estates Rum   **Title:** Umbrella, Swords, Shotgun

Art Directors: Sherrod Melvin, Zack Menna   **Copywriters:** Brad Emmett, Manor Gelber

Creative Director: Brad Emmett   **Executive Creative Director:** Sal DeVito   **Photographer:** Martin Wonnacott

When Appleton Estate Jamaica Rum approached us they wanted an ad campaign that was very specific. Appleton Estate wanted young, sophisticated spirits consumers to think differently about rum. They wanted spirits drinkers to know that "you no longer need to mix rum to enjoy rum." Not an easy task knowing that everyone loves their frozen daiquiri's and mojitos. After weeks of consuming numerous shots of Appleton, and killing numerous ideas, we finally discovered a new way to show drinkers how to enjoy Appleton Estate Rum, either neat or on the rocks. What really made this campaign idea work was how it visually demonstrated the ideal way to drink Appleton Estate Rum while expressing the high end position of Appleton Estate among other rums. But more importantly, it was fun, just the way a Jamaican rum should be. Rum is fun and should always be fun, even when communicating a more sophisticated and complex spirit like Appleton Estate. When the client gave us the assignment they never said this is the serious rum. They only said this is the rum that should never be mixed.

The Rum

THAT NEEDS NOTHING.

Ad Agency: bvk, Milwaukee, WI, USA | www.bvk.com   **Client:** Milwaukee County DA   **Title:** Bullet Candle
Art Director: Mike Scalise   **Creative Director:** Gary Mueller   **Photographer:** Glen Gyssler   **Copywriter:** Mike Holicek

Gun violence continues to be a serious problem in Milwaukee, as in many big cities around the country. The campaign — comprised of print, outdoor and bus shelters — attempts to keep the issue in the public consciousness by reminding everyone that gun violence is not an abstract problem. It's a problem that affects everyone in the community. And more importantly, that we must work together to find a solution.

The "bullet candle" visual was inspired by the idea of candlelight vigils that often mark the passing of a loved one. Readers are directed to a website called OneMilwaukee.org to learn more about current initiatives and what they can do to make a difference. Since the campaign was launched, more than 32,000 visitors have visited the website and there has been a double digit drop in gun deaths in the city of Milwaukee.

Ad Agency: bpg, Los Angeles, USA | www.bpgadvertising.com   **Client:** History   **Title:** Ice Road Truckers

Art Director: Masha Kupets   **Creative Director:** Steph Sebbag

History's highest rated show was back for its third season. The favorite guys of summer are driving on thinner roads, facing more danger and creating even more drama.

Our objective was to appeal to a broad male audience and the real life action aspect of the series. We created a 3D billboard of a truck that appears to be falling through ice. The headlights were practical and the use of a fog machine created smoke that billowed out of the exhaust pipes. There were only two boards created — one along New York's Westside Highway; the other on Los Angeles' Sunset Boulevard.

The premiere was watched by 3 million total viewers, 1.9 million Adults 25-54 and 1.7 million Adults 18-49, up 19% and 13% respectively versus Season 2.

Ad Agency: KNARF, New York, USA | www.knarfny.com   **Client:** School of Visual Arts   **Title:** Loose-Leaf Paper Bike-Rack

Art Directors: William Wang, Jelani Curtis, Frank Anselmo, Jeseok Yi, Richard Wilde   **Copywriters:** Jelani Curtis, William Wang

Creative Directors: Jeseok Yi, Richard Wilde   **Executive Creative Director:** Frank Anselmo

Pedestrians are inspired to see the world from a different perspective to remind them that creativity can happen anywhere and everywhere. Loose-leaf notebook pages made of heavy-duty 3M anti-slip vinyl were affixed on sidewalks beneath bike-racks. This created the illusion of classic loose-leaf notebook binders. The heavy-duty vinyl loose-leaf notebook pages were approximately 8 feet by 12 feet and were specifically designed to custom-fit the four-ring style bike racks commonly found in New York City.

Ad Agency: Clarity Coverdale Fury, Minneapolis, USA | www.ccf-ideas.com   **Client:** Red Gold   **Title:** Red Gold Truck

Executive Creative Director: Jac Coverdale   **Photographer:** Steve Umland

Red Gold's fleet of trucks deliver Red Gold Tomatoes to cities throughout its markets. We designed the truck graphics to raise brand awareness and reinforce the notion that Red Gold canned tomatoes have that fresh, just-picked flavor.

Ad Agency: Pyper Paul + Kenney, Tampa, FL, USA | www.pyperpaul.com   **Client:** Jailhouse Fire   **Title:** Hot Sauce Warning Sign Stickers
Art Directors: Kris Gregoire, Aaron Riney   **Associate Creative Director:** Michael Schillig   **Copywriter:** Michael Schillig   **Executive Creative Director:** Tom Kenney

We couldn't think of a better way to promote a new hot sauce created by inmates of the Hillsborough County jail then with a series of adhesive stickers that mimicked real warning labels. We placed these stickers in a variety of different settings around town in order to get people's attention and reinforce that this fiery hot sauce was packing a lot of heat and could only be purchased online.

This was one of a series of stickers that mimicked real warning labels, which we placed in a variety of different settings in order to get people's attention and reinforce that this hot sauce was created by jail inmates and can be purchased online.

This was one of a series of stickers that mimicked real warning labels, which we placed in a variety of different settings in order to get people's attention and reinforce that this hot sauce was created by jail inmates and can be purchased online.

Ad Agency: Colle + McVoy, Minneapolis, USA | www.collemcvoy.com   Client: Minnesota State Lottery   Title: Monopoly Hotel

Art Director: Dustin Black   Copywriter: John Neerland   Creative Director: Dave Keepper   Executive Creative Director: Mike Caguin

When we got the assignment to launch a Monopoly-themed scratch game, we knew that to break through it had to be markedly different from all the other work produced for Monopoly-licensed games. So, to connect players with the idea of winning big, we looked to two Monopoly icons for our imagery: the mustache and the red hotel. And then we made them huge.

Ad Agency: KNARF, New York, USA | www.knarfny.com   **Client:** School of Visual Arts   **Title:** Push The Envelope

Art Directors: Frank Anselmo, Jayson Atienza   **Copywriters:** Frank Anselmo, Jayson Atienza

Creative Directors: Jayson Atienza, Richard Wilde   **Executive Creative Director:** Frank Anselmo

ASSIGNMENT

The School of Visual Arts has a reputation for producing creative talent who have truly pushed the envelope of creativity in Advertising, Design, Cartooning, Computer Art, Film, Fine Arts, Illustration, Interior Design, Photography, etc. The brief was to communicate this forward thinking tradition. The targets were teenagers and their parents who were shopping for colleges/universities in the competitive New York City market.

SOLUTION

Images of envelopes with custom engraved steel push-plates were installed on the school's doors. With these custom door installations, The School of Visual Arts students literally "Pushed The Envelope" as they entered and exited the buildings.

TRANSLATION

"Push The Envelope" is an American phrase which means to innovate, or go beyond commonly accepted boundaries.

RESULTS

The School received 242 more applications than the previous year.

PUSH

School of
VISUAL ARTS

Ad Agency: BCF, Virginia Beach, VA, USA | www.boomyourbrand.com   **Client:** Discovery Channel   **Title:** Biscuits Ad

Account Director: Eric Lonning   **Agency Producer:** Mandy Lui   **Art Director:** Keith Ireland

Copywriter: Kevin McCarthy   **Creative Director:** Keith Ireland   **Project Manager:** Laura Bolt

The Discovery Channel tasked BCF with creating ads to promote their new show, Iditarod: The Toughest Race on Earth. This program gives viewers an inside look at the Iditarod sled dog race, which takes place annually in Alaska. The famous sled dog race covers over 1,150 miles of harsh terrain, extreme cold and wind chills that can break even the strongest of wills. With the show's main focus on the amazing bond between the mushers and their 14-16 dogs, we were able to see how dependent the team was on each other. Without every member working as one, neither would survive the grueling trek.

Although a total team effort, we wanted to spotlight the dogs as the true rock stars of the race. Their unwavering commitment to the task at hand and to their musher was truly remarkable. By using comedic headlines and adding a little swagger to the overall messaging, we were able to give the audience insight into the insane commitment and sacrifice that is the Iditarod.

YOU WANT TRICKS?
MY DOGS BURN
10000
CALORIES A DAY.
KEEP YOUR BISCUITS.

THE TOUGHEST RACE ON EARTH
IDITAROD
WEDNESDAYS 9.30PM
Discovery CHANNEL

Ad Agency: bpg, Los Angeles, USA | www.bigpicturegroup.net   **Client:** Syfy   **Title:** Caprica   **Art Director:** Richard Rho   **Creative Director:** Steph Sebbag

Set 50 years before the events in Syfy's mega hit Battlestar Galactica, Caprica, the prequel, tells the story of the birth of the Cylons. The multifaceted storyline explores the moral dilemma of saving human lives by turning them into Cylons (robots). We developed a print campaign that piques interest with the universal metaphor of the forbidden fruit.

Our goal was to drive show awareness, appeal to a younger audience, broaden the audience outside of the core Syfy and Battlestar fan base and drive tune in. With a strategic marketing plan that extended past the first week of premiere, ratings grew each week.

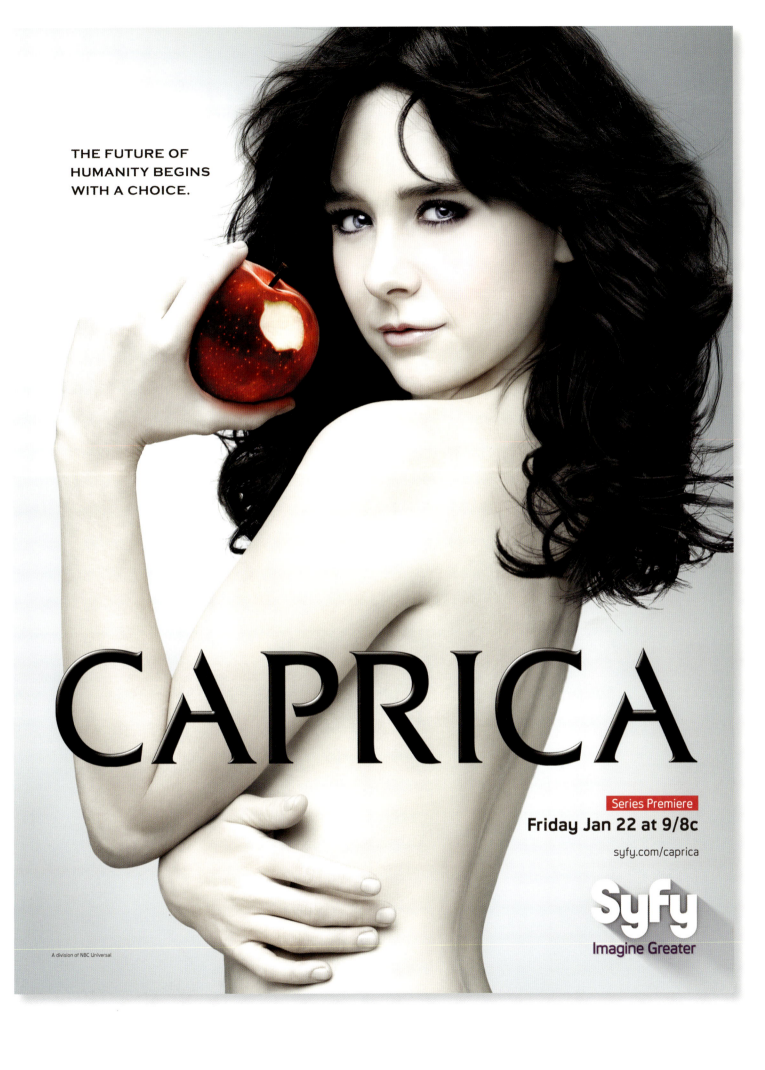

Ad Agency: BBDO West, San Francisco, USA | www.bbdo.com   **Client:** Comcast Sports Network   **Title:** Missing A's

Art Director: Lauren Weinblatt   **Copywriter:** Michael Barti   **Executive Creative Directors:** Jim Lesser, Jon Soto

San Francisco Bay Area sports fans needed to know that the Oakland A's baseball games would be broadcast on a new channel: Comcast SportsNet.

Surprising executions spelled the names of the Oakland A's star players with all of the letter "A's" missing. Viewers solved the puzzle when they found out they could "Find the A's on Comcast SportsNet." Billboards were placed on heavily traveled roads all around the Bay Area.

M TT HOLLID Y

J SON GI MBI

ERIC CH VEZ

Ad Agency: The Refinery, Burbank, CA, USA | www.therefinerycreative.com   **Client:** FOX Broadcasting Company   **Title:** 24 Season 8

Account Director: Jenny Jamin   **Art Directors:** Michael Valle, Sean Dunkerley, Jeff Birch, Josh Ecton   **Creative Directors:** Brad Hochberg, Adam Waldman

Designer: Moises Cisneros   **Executive Creative Directors:** Joe Earley, Michael Vamosy, Tom Morrissey   **Photographer:** Brian Bowen Smith   **Print Producer:** Diane Cooper

New York was to be the co-star to Kiefer Sutherland's character Jack Bauer for the advertising of season 8 of "24." Although it was not confirmed at the time, season eight for "24" was to be its final season. Fox (the client) wanted to showcase agent Jack Bauer in the world's most exciting city, New York. Several set ups were created for the photo shoot that showed Jack in action all over the city. The most challenging part of the job was editing all of the great material into a cohesive, dynamic campaign. The end result was multiple outdoor pieces that launched the show with exceptional ratings.

Ad Agency: Goodby, Silverstein & Partners, San Francisco, USA | www.gspsf.com   **Client:** Comcast   **Title:** Dream Big

Art Director: Stefan Copiz   **Creative Directors:** Jamie Barrett, Stefan Copiz, Chris Ford   **Copywriters:** Chris Ford, Paul Charney, Ryan Hoercher

This Comcast Town poster was part of a larger integrated Campaign for Comcast's TV, phone and Internet products. Working off a series of six animated television commercials, the poster directed users to comcasttown.com where they could build their own apartment, complete with big screen TV, computer and telephone. Users could also compete in a design contest, visit other users apartments, explore the products and showcase their living spaces via Facebook.

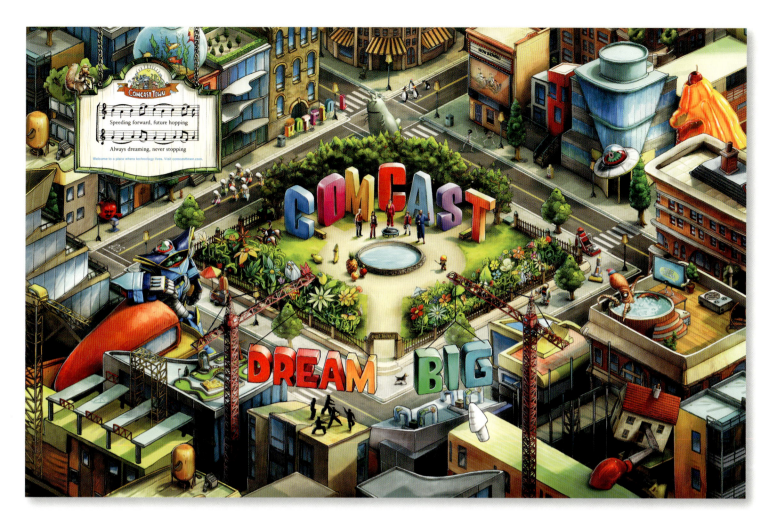

Ad Agency: TAXI CANADA INC, Calgary, Canada | www.taxi.ca	**Client:** PC Medic	**Title:** PC Medic Blue Screen of Death Campaign
Account Director: Ginny Wetmore	**Art Director:** Kelsey Horne **Creative Director:** Trent Burton	**Print Producer:** Marsha Walters **Copywriter:** Nick Asik

ASSIGNMENT

The object here is was to raise awareness that just because your PC's data is gone, it doesn't mean it's GONE. PC Medic specializes in retrieving your lost data.

APPROACH

How do we create compelling work that speaks to data recovery without resorting to standard clichés? And how do we do it in print?

BIG IDEA

What if the PC itself delivered the message. Even better, what if we used the PC "Screen of Death" as our canvas to relay that message. By laying out a series of outrageous ways one could retrieve their data, it was almost as if we we're having the PC taunt our consumers, with PC Medic being the solution.

RESULTS

The client was thrilled with how the work turned out and has seen a definite uptick in business and positive word of mouth as a result.

I know we were doing your taxes, but since those files don't exist anymore I have a
better idea. Don't do your taxes. Seriously, just don't do them.

WHAT'S_THE_WORST_THAT_CAN_HAPPEN?

Sure the feds might come after you and charge you for tax evasion. But not if you have
a plan. Here's what you're going to do. You're going to pack a suitcase with enough
clothes for a week. Then you're going to wake up tomorrow just like any other day, kiss
your wife and kids goodbye and go to work. Then you're going to drive right past the
office, head south and don't stop driving until you're in Mexico.

Think about it. It's just you, the open road and your fake beard blowing in the wind.
When you arrive your new name is Juan Pablo Ramirez and your father died in the war.
If they ask which war, throw them off by listing Taco Bell menu items and then
run away like, well, like you're a fugitive from justice, which you are.

Live as a drifter in Mexico

*** until your family assumes you're dead and more importantly until good old Revenue
Canada assumes you're dead. Then you can return to your old life, explain to your
children daddy was working over-overtime and they should call you Juan now, and you'll
never pay taxes again.

GET_YOUR_FILES_BACK. CALL_PC_MEDICS_AT_403_606_7234

So all your family photos are gone. What do I mean gone? I mean you'll never see the
pictures of your sweet little girl's first birthday or your son's adorable first steps
ever again.

THEY'RE_GONE_FOREVER.

But don't worry about it. Family photos are a dime a dozen. Every picture frame comes
with one. But you're thinking, "the family in the frame looks nothing like my family."
Which is true—before the plastic surgery.

But hey, maybe you don't feel right about putting your seven-year-old under the knife,
and that's perfectly fine.Because there's another way to get your photos back. Recreate
them. Re-invite the guests from seven years ago, strap birthday hats on the kids and
even though it might be hard to bring Sparky back from where he 'ran away' to, simply
point, shoot and

POOF! Your memories are back.

*** And when people ask why your seven year old is blowing out the candles on
her 'baby's first birthday' cake, just tell them she has mild Benjamin Button disease.
It's that easy.

GET_YOUR_FILES_BACK. CALL_PC_MEDICS_AT_403_606_7234

Ad Agency: Apple, Cupertino, CA, USA | www.apple.com   **Client:** Apple   **Title:** nano Poster   **Creative Director:** Apple Graphic Design

Retail posters for the new iPod nano showcasing two of the new features: a video camera and a shiny new polished aluminum finish.

We took a macro view and manipulated the arrangement of the product, transforming nanos into camera apertures. This approach showcases the product, and the element of surprise delights the viewer.

iPod nano

Ad Agency: Goodby, Silverstein & Partners, San Francisco, USA | www.gspsf.com   **Client:** Hewlett Packard   **Title:** Caution, Beware

Art Director: Ryan Meis   **Creative Directors:** Steve Simpson, Brian Gunderson, John Park   **Designer:** Ryan Meis   **Photographer:** Zachary Scott   **Copywriter:** John Park

The brief for the ads was simple and, unusual for advertising, based on truth: Original HP Inks are in fact far more reliable than the refills people often buy. That said, the product itself is mundane. To give our message some heat, we found inspiration in the energy and directness of early 20th century PSA posters. All the art work was built practically, which we thought helped update the universe these things usually live in.

Ad Agency: Goodby, Silverstein & Partners, San Francisco, USA | www.gspsf.com   **Client:** Hewlett Packard   **Title:** Caution, Beware

Art Director: Ryan Meis   **Creative Directors:** Steve Simpson, Brian Gunderson, John Park   **Designer:** Ryan Meis   **Photographer:** Zachary Scott   **Copywriter:** John Park

CAUTION:
HIDDEN COSTS.
BARGAIN BLACK TONERS COST UP TO
2X MORE OVER TIME THAN ORIGINAL HP TONER.

AMERICA'S #1 BRAND IS AMERICA'S #1 VALUE

1 in 3 bargain toners leak or fail while Original HP Toner delivers unmatched quality for far less long-term cost. Don't be fooled by imitations. Visit HP.COM/TONER

hp

HIT **PRINT**
INTELLIGENTLY

BEWARE:
1 IN 3 BARGAIN TONERS LEAK OR FAIL.

TONER TONER

AMERICA'S #1 BRAND IS AMERICA'S #1 VALUE

Original HP Toner delivers unmatched quality, time and time again. In fact, bargain black toners can cost up to 2X more over time than Original HP Toner. Don't be fooled by imitations. Visit HP.COM/TONER

hp

HIT **PRINT**
INTELLIGENTLY

Ad Agency: KNARF, New York, USA | www.knarfny.com   **Client:** School of Visual Arts   **Title:** Don't Depend On Luck

Art Director: Frank Anselmo   **Copywriter:** Duc Nguyen   **Creative Director:** Richard Wilde   **Executive Creative Director:** Frank Anselmo

BACKGROUND

The School of Visual Arts has many creative departments rated amongst the top in the world. The goal was to communicate that choosing any other school is a compromise and you'd be taking a gamble — hence the line: "Don't Depend On Luck." The ironic, yet truthful details surrounding the animals featured served as metaphors to communicate the strategy. The posters stood out amongst the many cliché recruitment posters normally seen done for schools.

TURKEY

Behold this unfortunate flightless bird, rendered asexual and bred by artificial insemination. Reduced to an industrial commodity and packed into plants by the thousands with breasts so swollen from genetic manipulation that their legs collapse beneath them. Yet, millions of people take joy in finding the poor turkey's wishbone, believing it will somehow bring luck. But what exactly about this misbegotten bird is so lucky? If it was lucky, it would have been an eagle. Don't depend on luck. Create Your Own Future. School of Visual Arts.

HORSE

Equine nobility. Born to run free, but tamed by man and shod in iron. Led to field by peasants and broken by the plow. Or raced on the tracks of kings only to shatter upon the hard dirt. And finally, to slaughter and the most ignoble of ends, as food for lesser beasts. Yet, in spite of this misery, the horseshoe, the very symbol of a horse's servitude is still seen as a vessel of good fortune. But the horse knows different. It knows that the horseshoe leads to many things, but good luck is never one of them. Don't depend on luck. Create Your Own Future. School of Visual Arts.

RABBIT

Look down the food chain, down near the very bottom where life is most precarious and you'll find him. The prince of a thousand enemies. Set upon by fox and wolf. Caught in the talons of both hawk and owl. Laid low by the arrows of man. And yet, the grisly tradition of severing the poor rabbit's foot for luck endures. As if the very foot that couldn't even save its own master from a ghastly end, could somehow bring its new owner good fortune. Don't depend on luck. Create Your Own Future. School of Visual Arts.

Behold this unfortunate flightless bird, rendered asexual and bred by artificial insemination. Reduced to an industrial commodity and packed into plants by the thousands with breasts so swollen from genetic manipulation that their legs collapse beneath them. Yet, millions of people take joy in finding the poor turkey's wishbone, believing it will somehow bring luck. But what exactly about this misbegotten bird is so lucky? If it was lucky, it would have been an eagle. Don't depend on luck. Create Your Own Future.

School of Visual Arts

sva.edu

Equine nobility. Born to run free, but tamed by man and shod in iron. Led to field by peasants and broken by the plow. Or raced on the tracks of kings only to shatter upon the hard dirt. And finally, to slaughter and the most ignoble of ends, as food for lesser beasts. Yet, in spite of this misery, the horseshoe, the very symbol of a horse's servitude is still seen as a vessel of good fortune. But the horse knows different. It knows that the horseshoe leads to many things, but good luck is never one of them. Don't depend on luck. Create Your Own Future.

School of Visual Arts

sva.edu

Ad Agency: Goodby, Silverstein & Partners, San Francisco, USA | www.gspsf.com   **Client:** Hardly Strictly Bluegrass   **Title:** Hardly Strictly Bluegrass

Art Director: Claude Shade   **Creative Director:** Jeff Goodby   **Photographer:** Claude Shade

The Hardly Strictly Bluegrass Festival has been going on for nine years now and is the largest festival of its kind in the USA. It was originally called the Bluegrass Festival for two years and at the time featured 20 bands. Since then, it has grown to include various musical acts, not only those that are in the Bluegrass category — hence the name change to Hardly Strictly Bluegrass. Now acts such as Robert Plant, Elvis Costello, Dolly Parton, Jeff Tweedy, Willy Nelson and comedian Steve Martin have played there.

Ad Agency: Muller Bressler Brown, Kansas City, MO, USA | www.mbbagency.com   **Client:** Kansas International Film Festival   **Title:** Movies Up Close

Art Director: Amy Young   **Copywriter:** Tommy Donoho   **Creative Director:** Shan Neely   **Photographer:** Colby Lysne

ASSIGNMENT

The Kansas International Film Festival not only brings movies to Kansas that otherwise wouldn't get screened in the area, but it's also their mission to bring as many filmmakers, actors and producers in town for autographs and Q&A sessions. We were asked to find a creative way to get that message across.

APPROACH

What's challenging for a film festival in the Midwest? What's not challenging about it? The name alone, "Kansas International Film Festival" can incite laughter in some and skepticism in others. We had to convince moviegoers that the festival was legitimate and very approachable, as well as being their one chance a year to meet movie makers locally.

THE BIG IDEA

The ultimate solution was to physically demonstrate just how close moviegoers are to the movie-making process. We came up with three different cliché movie scenes and inserted the everyday moviegoer into each situation.

RESULTS

Our clients (the Board of Directors) are avid moviegoers. They got a kick out of the cliché movie scenes we came up with and thought we did a great job connecting the film festival to the traditional movie going experience. By doing so, Kansans saw the festival as an opportunity to not only see great movies, but to meet the people behind them as well. We increased their individual ticket sales 10% and increased sales of week long festival passes by 50%!

Glenwood Arts Theatre
9575 Metcalf
SEPTEMBER
18 THRU 24
kansasfilm.com
kansas
INTERNATIONAL
fiLm
festival
see the movies. Meet the people behind them.

Movies up close.

Glenwood Arts Theatre
9575 Metcalf
SEPTEMBER
18 THRU 24
kansasfilm.com
kansas
INTERNATIONAL
fiLm
festival
see the movies. Meet the people behind them.

Movies up close.

Ad Agency: Lindsay, Stone & Briggs, Madison, WI, USA ¦ www.lsb.com   **Client:** Jazz at Five   **Title:** Jet Pack

Art Director: Matt Johanning   **Creative Director:** Bill Winchester   **Copywriter:** Lee Schmidt

ASSIGNMENT

Our job? Build awareness for Jazz at 5, a summer concert series that takes its name from the 5 p.m. start time of every performance. These outdoor concerts, performed in the shadow of the Wisconsin state capitol, bring together local fans and nationally recognized jazz artists.

APPROACH

Jazz does not currently enjoy the popularity of other music genres. So how do we generate interest? In a college town with a large population of young people who prefer pop, rock and hip hop, how do we get them to turn out to hear live jazz?

THE BIG IDEA

We created a humorous poster campaign that leverages a key insight: jazz musicians improvise like no one else. Improvisation is what makes jazz different and cool. Our campaign takes a tongue-in-cheek jab at other ways people improvise. Of course, when other people improvise they don't do it very well. Only jazz musicians can improvise and get it right. Merchants on State Street, the main street stretching between the university and the capitol, placed our posters in their windows.

RESULTS

The four Jazz at 5 concerts were exceptionally well attended. People, young and old, lined sidewalks and streets to hear live jazz. A fifth concert has been added to the 2010 concert series.

IMPROVISATION.
Best left to musicians.
JAZZ AT FIVE
FREE CONCERT SERIES
AUG 5 - AUG 26 • 100 STATE STREET • jazzat5.org • 608-310-4462
5

Ad Agency: BradfordLawton, LLC, San Antonio, TX, USA | www.bradfordlawton.com

Account Directors: Tony Diamond, Lindsay Crowell

Client: Lewis Energy

Title: Lewis Fly-In Poster

Designers: Bradford Lawton, Josh Zapata

This year, Rod and Kim Lewis celebrated their 15th annual Fly-In event and asked us to design an invitation to commemorate the anniversary. We created this poster to be mailed to guests in poster tubes. Over 30 Warbirds participate in the fly-in and air show. The most famous of which is a World War II-vintage P-38 Lightning called "Glacier Girl," part of the legendary "Lost Squadron" recovered from under 268 feet of ice in Greenland. We created the P-38 silhouette in the clouds to subtly pay tribute to Glacier Girl and the Lost Squadron.

THE 2010 LEW**15** FLY-IN
FIFTEENTH ANNIVERSARY

MARCH 27, 2010 10AM - 5PM | EL JARDIN RANCH, ENCINAL, TEXAS

Ad Agency: Lloyd & Company Advertising, Inc., New York, USA | www.lloydandco.com   **Client:** Jil Sander   **Title:** Jil Sander Spring/Summer 2009   **Art Directors:** Douglas Lloyd, Jason Evans

A series of graphic black and white silhouettes that reference both the photo-manipulation of Man Ray and the elongation of form attributed to African tribal sculpture.

JIL SANDER

Ad Agency: TBWA\Barcelona, Spain | www.tbwa.es

Art Director: Jordi Rins

Creative Director: Miquel Sales

Client: Adidas

Copywriter: Albert Calzina

Title: mi adidas

Photographer: Ramon Serrano

ASSIGNMENT

With "mi adidas," Adidas launched a new online platform allowing their customers the ability to customize their favorite Adidas sneakers.

APPROACH

The challenges was to create a striking and simple image (the qualities of a good design poster) with the product.

THE BIG IDEA

The solution was create a sneaker made of paint because choosing your shoe color was the most pivotal part of the "mi adidas" process.

RESULTS

The client likes it very much. In response to this poster, Adidas international has created a campaign around the concept of our "mi adidas" advertisements.

create your adidas

Ad Agency: MD70, New York, USA | www.md70.com   **Client:** Mr. Nils   **Title:** FW10   **Creative Director:** Johan Holmstrom

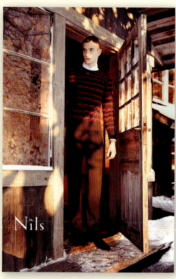

Mr. Nils embodies effortless cool. Being a little rough around the edges only makes him look better. He doesn't need to spend an hour in front of the mirror striving for perfection. Perfection is boring. He knows that he'll look great in whatever he throws on. The time spent getting ready is time that could be spent living. He stands firmly between two worlds. The city is his, but he needs the peace and silence of the countryside from time to time: a Nordic approach to life.

To reflect this the FW10 campaign was shot in Mr. Nilsson's hometown of Darlarna in Northern Sweden. We sought to draw directly from Mr. Nilsson's heritage and reflect the set of beliefs that clothing for the country is as vital as attire for city life.

Mr Nils

Ad Agency: Butler, Shine, Stern & Partners, Sausalito, CA, USA | www.bssp.com   **Client:** Sorel   **Title:** Vogue Legs, Vogue Model

Art Director: Carrie Ammermann   **Executive Creative Directors:** John Butler, Mike Shine, Tom Coates   **Copywriter:** Aimee Lehto   **Photographer:** Erik Almas

ASSIGNMENT

Our assignment was to change perceptions of the Sorel brand and introduce Sorel to an entirely new consumer — the fashion forward, savvy and selective Millennial female. After decades of making warm, waterproof performance winter footwear, people knew Sorel as that functional winter boot that never needed to be replaced. Sorel wanted to take a step off of the mountain and into the fashion world. Our assignment was to position Sorel as footwear that delivers both fashion and function: a utilitarian chic look that is perfect for the modern, urban woman.

APPROACH

Sorel had no awareness as a fashion footwear brand. And while Sorel's heritage helped us maintain our equity in functional product, it was a hindrance in establishing the brand in the fashion space. We needed to make a bold statement about our role as a fashion brand without losing the positive associations of the past.

THE BIG IDEA

To announce this step in a more fashionable direction, we created these print ads to run in Vogue during the fall and winter. The ads juxtapose the wilderness, traditionally associated with Sorel, and the urban landscape that will be the stomping ground for the next generation of Sorel boots.

RESULTS

Increased sell-through was attributed to the total campaign. Aggressive sales goals have been established and the marketing budget has doubled for 2010 as a result of Sorel's 2009 success. Also, a Vista study was conducted with Vogue magazine that showed Sorel had very high ad awareness and brand association, particularly for a first time appearance in print. We also built new awareness with a fashionable audience (52% not previously aware of Sorel) and enhanced perceptions of Sorel among both already aware and newly aware audiences. Specifically, Sorel is more stylish now, Sorel is a brand for me, Sorel makes stylish boots for women and Sorel blends fashion and function.

Après anything. **SOREL**

sorel.com

Ad Agency: The Refinery, Minneapolis, USA | www.therefineryonline.com   **Client:** Screen Gems   **Title:** Priest

Art Director: Sean Dunkerley   **Account Director:** Jenny Jamin

Creative Directors: Brad Hochberg, Adam Waldman   **Executive Creative Directors:** Jim Fredrick, Tiffany Jamison

The object of Priest was to announce to the world at San Diego Comic-Con 2009 that the famed graphic novel was being made into a movie. Screen Gems (our client) had a very specific idea on what they wanted to see. A tattoo needed to be placed on Paul Bettany's face, (the main hero in the movie) to signify that his role was high priest in a world of vampires and those who battle them. The resulting image was simple, dramatic and created much buzz and anticipation amongst fan boys. Our client was satisfied.

PRIEST†

2010

Ad Agency: Goodby, Silverstein & Partners, San Francisco, USA | www.goodbysilverstein.com   **Client:** Quaker   **Title:** Quaker Magazine
Art Director: Cris Logan   **Creative Directors:** Jamie Barrett, Will McGinness   **Copywriter:** Jamie Barrett

ASSIGNMENT

For as long as most people can remember, Quaker has been touting the cholesterol-fighting benefits of oats. While this is certainly an important message, Quaker felt it was getting a bit dated. To counter this, we created simple telegraphic images that used metaphors of power and energy to convey the positive effects of having a healthy Quaker breakfast. We paired this with the tag "Go humans go" — a declaration of encouragement during one of the most difficult economic times in history.

APPROACH

Go humans go. This was more than a tagline. It was a rallying cry intended to speak to people on a level deeper than what a consumable product could typically satisfy. We wanted to move the brand out of their packaged goods comfort zone and engage their core audience in a way they had never done before. And, of course, win over new customers. We set out to make it a socially relevant brand—to dimensionalize the iconic Quaker Man in a way that excited consumers.

THE BIG IDEA

Our ultimate solution was simple, actually. All print, OOH and TV executions dramatized the positive energy of Quaker Oats. It's clean fuel. We built a campaign out of visual metaphors for clean energy, like the coiled spring ad you see here.

RESULTS

Because the campaign was so visually arresting, the OOH (similar executions as the print) worked very hard for the campaign. In the regional markets where we ran the full OOH plan on top of the national TV and print, sales lifted by 5%. The campaign was also a success in the sense that Quaker became a point of chatter all over the world. Message boards and social media sites buzzed about the sometimes mysterious, sometimes cute, yet always playful images. Go humans go became a target of parody both online and via street artists — always a sign of pop culture ubiquity.

Put a little spring in your step.
With Quaker Chewy bars made from whole grain oats.

Go humans go

Ad Agency: Baily Lauerman, Lincoln, NE, USA | www.baileylauerman.com   **Client:** ConAgra Foods   **Title:** ConAgra "Food Love" Posters

Art Directors: Ron Sack, Dave Markes   **Creative Director:** Marty Amsler   **Photographers:** Bob Ervin, Mike Kleveter   **Copywriter:** Rainbow Rowell

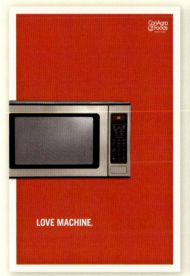

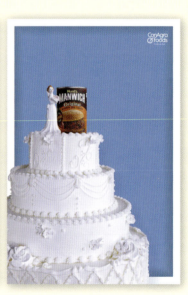

Part of a campaign introducing ConAgra Foods' new logo and "Food You Love" positioning line to ConAgra employees. The campaign asked employees to think of every ConAgra food as the object of someone's affection.

IF YOU LOVE SOMETHING, SET IT FREE.

Agency: Pyper Paul + Kenney, Tampa, FL, USA | www.pyperpaul.com   **Client:** Jailhouse Fire   **Title:** Lethal, Bottle Bomber

Art Director: Tom Kenney   **Associate Creative Director:** Michael Schillig   **Copywriter:** Michael Schillig   **Executive Creative Director:** Tom Kenney   **Photographer:** Aaron Riney

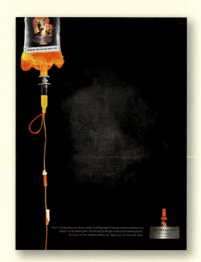

This poster was designed to first and foremost grab people's attentions through the use of a very powerful, even somewhat controversial visual. We wanted to play off the unique attributes of the brand since this hot sauce was actually created by jail inmates. We also wanted to convey that "No Escape" Hot Sauce is extremely hot and is only available for purchase online.

YOU HAVE OVER 10,000 TASTE BUDS.
HOPE AT LEAST A FEW OF THEM SURVIVE.

Pity the poor, little, innocent taste buds that get caught in the path of this fiery new hot sauce. No Escape is created by inmates with an explosive blend of hand-grown peppers and spices. The taste is to die for. So get some at your own risk.

All profits support equipment and supplies for inmate programs.

jailhousefire
Created with conviction.
www.jailhousefire.org

Ad Agency: Cramer Krasselt, Milwaukee, WI, USA | www.c-k.com   **Client:** Spice Islands   **Title:** Cinnamon, Bay Leaves, Dill

Art Director: Jim Root   **Copywriter:** Sandy DerHovsepian   **Creative Directors:** Chris Jacobs, Michael Fazende   **Photographer:** Jeff Salzer

Not all spices are created equal.

Spice Islands is a line of eclectic, premium spices available on the grocery store spice aisle. With limited distribution and an even more limited advertising budget, they compete with huge, ubiquitous brands like McCormick. The fact that Spice Islands cost a little more makes the task even more difficult, especially during a down economy where consumers are cutting back and trying to make every penny count.

The job, in our minds, was to differentiate Spice Islands from the McCormick's of the world by making the brand stand apart in terms of it's authentic flavors. Historically, Spice Islands has gone to the ends of the earth to source its spices, from places like South Vietnam for Saigon Cinnamon and Madagascar for the finest vanilla beans. As a result, Spice Islands spices are not mass produced, but done so with an artisan's expertise.

The bottom line is that although a bit more expensive, Spice Islands spices are "worth it." That authentic, artisan quality had to be delivered at every consumer touch point and with a miniscule budget. Where McCormick would wield a hammer with a huge television plan, Spice Islands would need a sharper nail and rely on print and online.

As a result of running our "Difference" print campaign during a key advertising period in January 2010, brand awareness increased by 9 points, which was the largest increase among all spice brands. And despite a down economy, Spice Islands is now driving sales growth in the premium spice category, up 8.5% from a year ago. All of this points to the impact the Spice Islands campaign is creating in the marketplace.

Dill Weed
IS MOST FLAVORFUL WHEN IT BLOOMS.

SO WHY IS OURS THE ONLY DILL WITH BLOSSOMS?

most flavorful

less flavorful

fig. 1 dill weed

Look closely. See those tiny yellow flecks in our dill weed? They're the yellow blossoms that appear when dill reaches its peak of flavor. We harvest them during the three-day window when dill is extra dilly. Waiting for the right moment takes patience a lot of other dill producers don't have. As a result, their dill has a duller, slightly grassy taste. No grilled salmon deserves that. Next time you're at the store, look for our California dill weed with the flavorful little yellow buds. It's just one of our distinctive Spice Islands flavors. Learn more at spiceislands.com.

{ WHAT THE WORLD TASTES LIKE™ }

SPICE ISLANDS
EST. 1941
DILL WEED
NET WT 0.9 OZ (26 GRAMS)

Ad Agency: Colle + McVoy, Minneapolis, USA | www.collemcvoy.com   **Client:** Nestle Purina   **Title:** Rottweiler, Yorkie

Art Directors: Derek Till, Zara Gonzalez   **Copywriter:** Brian Ritchie   **Creative Director:** Eric Husband   **Executive Creative Director:** Mike Caguin   **Photographer:** Jonathan Chapman

ASSIGNMENT

Our charge in creating a new brand campaign for Purina Pro Plan was to convince breeders, handlers and owners that feeding a dog the right food is a huge part of a dog's success in the world of dog shows. The campaign was to demonstrate the important role nutrition plays in a dog's success while also acknowledging the role the breeder plays in that success.

APPROACH

Our insight was based around the idea of defining success. We knew that whether you're a professional or an enthusiast, everyone has goals they aspire to reach. The challenge was to serve up these goals without feeling elitist or catering too much to the lowest common denominator.

THE BIG IDEA

Knowing that everyone's definition of success is different, we created a new inspirational theme line that all could personalize to their own individual goals: This could be the year. Whether the goal is to win Westminster or just to enter a dog show for the first time, this campaign encourages everyone to dream of what the coming year has in store. Using a photo journalistic approach to the imagery, we set out to capture these beautiful dogs in their natural environment, the show ring. By shooting these dogs as if they were professional athletes, we were able to capture the energy, intensity and passion those involved in the world of dog shows know all too well.

RESULTS

The campaign has been an overwhelming success. In total, 17 different print ads were created, tailored to breed specific publications and their audiences. As a result, Pro Plan has continued its dominance over all other brands of food among top breeders. Currently, 89 out of the top 100 show dogs rated by the American Kennel Club are fed Purina Pro Plan. A staggering number that has helped extend the reach of the brand to breeders who aspire to see great results out of their dogs as well.

This could be the year
A DIVA IS BORN.

PURINA
PRO PLAN

This could be the year
OUR GAIT BECOMES A SWAGGER.

PURINA
PRO PLAN

Ad Agency: JWT Sydney, Australia | www.jwt.com.au   **Client:** Nestlé   **Title:** Club Chocolate Intense Pleasure   **Art Director:** Blair Kimber

Associate Creative Director: John Lam   **Designer:** Andrew van der Westhuyzen   **Executive Creative Director:** Andrew Fraser   **Copywriter:** Simon Armour

We all know that chocolate can elicit strong emotional responses. To relaunch Club, Nestle's dark chocolate range, JWT Sydney used Club to visualize the brain's neurological response to eating dark chocolate. A television commercial was a visualization of reactions throughout the entire eating experience and the print campaign featured key responses when the pleasure of eating chocolate was at its most intense.

STIR
SOMETHING
DEEP INSIDE

STIR
SOMETHING
DEEP INSIDE

Ad Agency: The Martin Agency, Richmond, VA, USA | www.martinagency.com   **Client:** John F. Kennedy Presidential Library & Museum   **Title:** Quarantine, Launch, Step

Account Director: Carrie Bird   **Art Director:** Brian Williams   **Creative Director:** Joe Alexander   **Print Producer:** Jenny Schoenherr   **Copywriter:** Wade Alger

2009 marked the 40th anniversary of the Apollo 11 moon landing — the realization of President John F. Kennedy's dream to land a man on the moon. The John F. Kennedy Presidential Library and Museum wanted to celebrate this initiative and drive traffic to the museum. A local print campaign utilized photos of the mission and the world's reactions as the historic event unfolded. All of these were tied together with lines that celebrated the achievement. These local directives were used as print, bus shelters and outdoor advertising.

July 20, 1969.
The world stops to watch one man take a walk.

The Moon Landing 40th Anniversary.
The JFK Library and Museum **jfklibrary.org**

Ad Agency: STUDIO INTERNATIONAL, Zagreb, Croatia | www.studio-international.com   **Client:** Museum Documentation Centre   **Title:** Museum

Art Director: Boris Ljubicic   **Designer:** Boris Ljubicic

ASSIGNMENT

Museum as a theme has been used in various ways. Posters mainly represent artifacts exhibited in a museum. The question was how to attract the attention of a public which normally doesn't go to museums.

APPROACH

Tourists do not want to waste too much time in museums, as they want to experience other things as well. Museums are the space of spiritual food. The famous McDonald's logo is a symbol of fast and cheap food. It is attractive and with its bright and warm colors it associates some ART works of the 20th century.

THE BIG IDEA

The word MUSEUM had been derived from the Logo. M is food for the eyes, something you have already seen and something promising. It is quite amusing when there is a McDonald's restaurant in the vicinity, as then there is an interaction of the people who consume one and the other. Museum gets a new public. Poster colors attract visitors in the vicinity. There is also a monochrome version, which is used in a wider space of the city.

RESULTS

The client wanted to attract more people into the museums, notably those who never visit it and young people. There are several reasons why most of the people do not visit the museums, with the exception of passionate art lovers. Museums are the places where we should consume culture. Number of visitors has increased and with that profit increased also..

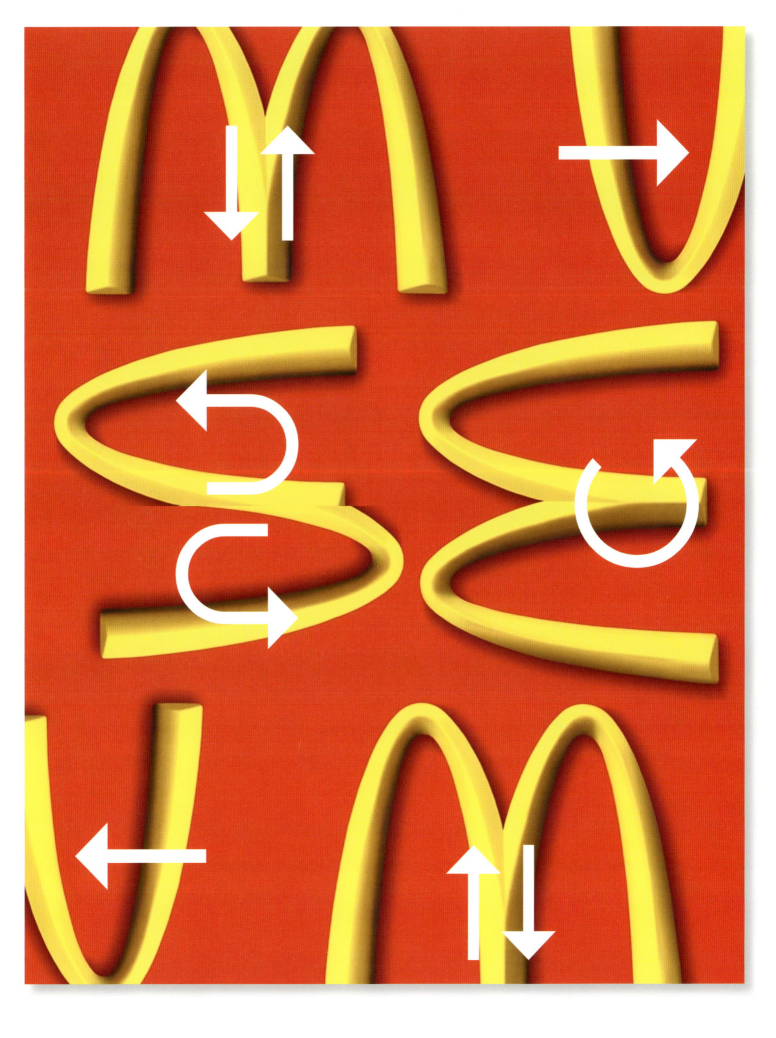

Ad Agency: The Martin Agency, Richmond, VA, USA | www.martinagency.com   Client: John F. Kennedy Presidential Library & Museum

Title: Millions, Flag, Launch   Account Director: Carrie Bird   Art Director: Brian Williams

Creative Director: Joe Alexander   Print Producer: Jenny Schoenherr   Copywriter: Wade Alger

2009 marked the 40th anniversary of the Apollo 11 moon landing, the realization of President John F. Kennedy's dream to land a man on the moon. In an address at Rice University on September 12, 1962, he boldly laid out his vision and rationale for the nation's space program.

Those words were the seeds that would ultimately flower seven years later in the historic mission Kennedy himself would never see. In order to connect his words to the event, we used archival imagery from the launch, landing and splashdown, and simply replaced salient objects from the scene with his words, allowing Kennedy's words to be visually central to the mission.

"We choose to go to the moon. We choose to go to the moon in this decade and do the other things, not because they are easy, but because they are hard... because that challenge is one that we are willing to accept, one we are unwilling to postpone, and one which we intend to win."

Some speeches change the world. Some take you to an entirely new one.

The Moon Landing 40th Anniversary. The JFK Library and Museum **jfklibrary.org**

Ad Agency: The Martin Agency, Richmond, VA, USA | www.martinagency.com   **Client:** John F. Kennedy Presidential Library & Museum   **Title:** Apollo 11 Launch

Account Director: Carrie Bird   **Art Director:** Brian Williams   **Creative Director:** Joe Alexander   **Print Producer:** Jenny Schoenherr   **Copywriter:** Wade Alger

As remarkable as space exploration is, it's almost as remarkable how desensitized we've become to its advances. We created a series of posters to draw people to our WeChooseTheMoon.org site that not only celebrated the mission, but also took you back to the late 1960s — when the lines between science and science fiction were blurred and anything seemed possible.

The poster series began with accurate renderings of the rocket, spacecraft and lander, which were then embellished with elements inspired by late 1960s fantasy art and semi-scientific and futurist posters and stamps.

Ad Agency: TBWA\RAAD, Dubai, United Arab Emirates | www.tbwaraad.com   **Client:** The Fridge   **Title:** Corporate Series

Design Director: Andrea Gruneberg   **Designers:** Breda Plavec, Kris Balerite

The Fridge is the only live, grassroots music venue filling the cultural void that is Dubai. But not enough people know about it. The Fridge needed to articulate its vision of building a genuine underground music scene by attracting the right audience. Dubai advertising is all glitz and glamour with superlatives and slick photography. Yet, The Fridge is located in a warehouse in a remote, industrial area. The challenge was to communicate the simple, genuine soul of The Fridge without going mainstream. The posters capture the feel of the venue: dark, organic, yet mysteriously different. The raw look, the hand-drawn typography keeps the place safe from trend chasers. 'Musical creatures' invite people to "find music" in the most unexpected place. As the posters spread amongst city's underground scene, the venue noted a steady increase in followers. And what was initially meant to be a poster became a give away for the culture-starved.

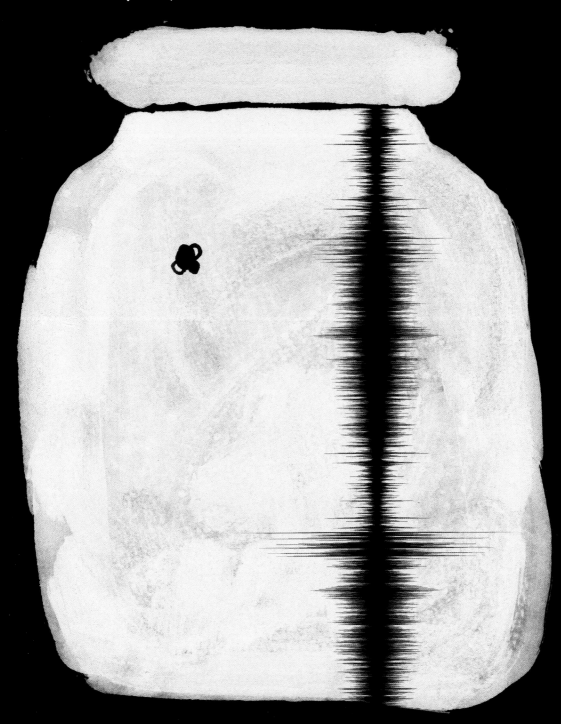

Ad Agency: MacLaren McCann Calgary, Canada | www.maclaren.com   **Client:** Recordland   **Title:** iPod posters   **Art Directors:** Mike Meadus, Mark Lovely
Creative Director: Mike Meadus   **Designer:** Mike Meadus   **Photographer:** Justen Lacoursiere   **Copywriters:** Nicolle Pittman, Sean Mitchell

Fast food, instant messaging, bullet trains — the developed world has no shortage of speed. But like any trend, there will always be people who gravitate to the opposite. Having 120 GB of digital music in your pocket is great, but we'll always have a soft spot for the sharp crackle and warm purr of a classic vinyl album played front to back at 33 RPM.

These iPod look alike posters, under closer inspection, are actually classic album covers and vinyl, and went up in December at a number of Calgary locations to remind people that Recordland is still one of the world's biggest resources for vinyl albums and hard-to-find music.

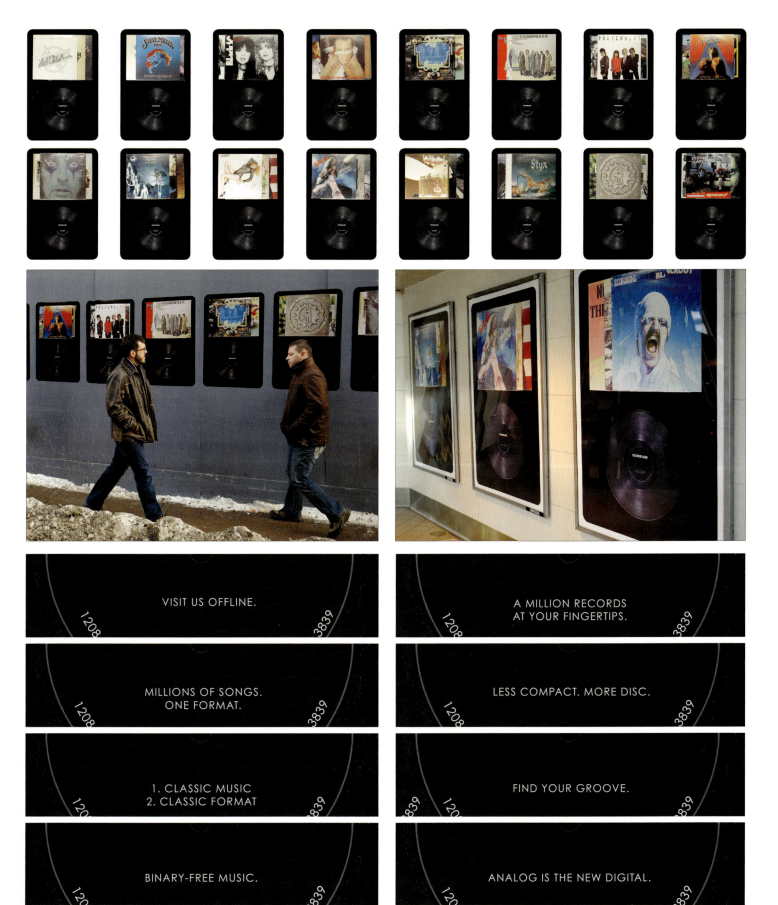

VISIT US OFFLINE.

MILLIONS OF SONGS.
ONE FORMAT.

1. CLASSIC MUSIC
2. CLASSIC FORMAT

BINARY-FREE MUSIC.

A MILLION RECORDS
AT YOUR FINGERTIPS.

LESS COMPACT. MORE DISC.

FIND YOUR GROOVE.

ANALOG IS THE NEW DIGITAL.

Ad Agency: TBWA\BRUSSELS, Belgium | www.tbwagroup.be   **Client:** Ambiance by Levis Paints (Akzo Nobel)   **Title:** Red Dress

Account Manager: Hadoum Ghassab   **Account Supervisor:** Christine Robie   **Advertiser's Supervisor:** Annick Teughels   **Art Director:** Alex Ameye   **Art Buyer:** Elly Laureys

Copywriter: Wilfrid Morin   **Creative Director:** Jan Macken   **Illustrator Photo-Retouching:** Magic Group Amsterdam/Marianne Gualtieri (TBWA\)   **Photographer:** Kurt Stallaert

Every year, Levis paints launches a range of trendy colors inspired by fashion designers: the Ambiance collection. Hence, the 'Fashion For Walls' signature.

FASHION FOR WALLS

New collection by Veronique Branquinho

Ad Agency: Karo Group Inc., Calgary, Canada ┊ www.karo.com		Client: Otterbottle Inc.		Title: Caps	
Account Director: Leigh Blakely	Art Director: Scott Shymko	Copywriters: Craig Reynolds, Phil Copithorne		Creative Director: Phil Copithorne	Photographer: Jean Perron

ASSIGNMENT

Otterbottle is a small, but growing player in the reusable beverage container category. Otterbottles are 100% stainless steel, BPA-free and more environmentally friendly when compared to some metal and all plastic container alternatives. Given these exceptional product qualities, Otterbottle easily attracts a strong following within the health food segment, but they wanted to broaden their audience. Our client asked us to deliver an ad that would cause average consumers to reassess and change ingrained behavior.

APPROACH

Otterbottle asked us to portray their product as a catalyst for change. To make this happen, we proposed to keep the messaging simple and high level. So, even though Otterbottles have many attractive aspects, our primary challenge was to show the most relevant product benefit to the average consumer of bottled water — its reusability.

THE BIG IDEA

Every year, over 2.5 million tons of plastic is used in the production of bottled water worldwide. Often, the water put in those bottles is of equal or poorer quality than the locally available tap water. Yet, perhaps most disturbing of all, a significant portion of those plastic containers never gets recycled. With millions of used water bottles going into landfills each year, our execution is a simple yet powerful demonstration of the positive environmental impact just one stainless steel Otterbottle can make.

RESULTS

The ad was a hit with both the client and consumers. As a result, Otterbottle experienced measurable increase in orders and even attracted several new retailers into its distribution chain due to consumer inquiries.

PROMOTING A PLASTIC-FREE WORLD

Otterbottle

Ad Agency: Brian Kuhlmann Studio, Chicago, USA | www.briankuhlmann.com   **Client:** Ellington Fans   **Title:** It's So You   **Art Directors:** George Reynolds, Melody Tarver

The "It's So You" images were created to continue the mood and taste begun by the client's previous campaign. I was selected because of my particular use of lighting as well as my ability to create and capture beautiful moments. Working in the studio, I needed to create three unique settings that communicated comfort and familiarity, as well as intrigue and drama. Each set was based on a well-known style — the Victorian Antoinette, the classic Audrey Hepburn and the sleek modern — but approached each with a fresh perspective to add contemporary flair. The fan shadow, though simple in theory, proved to be troublesome in pre-production. Fans were provided by the client, which we used to make scaled-down 2D props by tracing the blade and unit shapes. These scale "fans" were wrangled by an assistant, adding an element of spontaneity to the shoot: it kept everyone on their toes and working to capture the perfect shots. By forgoing digital post-production and creating the shadow on-set, we created a lush and dramatic environment with a hint of fantasy to it that invites the viewer to step inside and experience the feeling.

Sometimes I feel I was born two hundred years too late.

It's so you. **ELLINGTON**
EllingtonFans.com

*To me, simplicity means picking one thing
and giving it room to shine.*

It's so you. **ELLINGTON**
EllingtonFans.com

Ad Agency: JWT Chile, Santiago, Chile | www.jwt.com   **Client:** Scrabble   **Title:** Scrabble   **Art Director:** Matías Lecaros   **Creative Directors:** Matías Lecaros, Sergio Rosati
Copywriter: Matías Lecaros   **Executive Creative Director:** Leo Farfan   **Illustrator:** Boris Berstel   **Photographer:** Cristián Gastello

ASSIGNMENT

With a very minimal budget, the client requested a campaign to promote the game Scrabble, with emphasis on the nature of the game itself: form words with random letters.

APPROACH

Given the low budget, the challenge was to do something very public, so as to compensate for the lack of exhibition opportunities, with an idea that was so remarkable that it calls our attention.

THE BIG IDEA

The big idea was to use only fractionated images (without words) to show the essence of the game, which is to build words with random letters.

RESULTS

Notable exhibition and free coverage in different media, given the large number of creative awards that were obtained. While it did not generate significant revenue, it contributed much to the reputation of the brand, as a witty and eye-catching game.

SCRABBLE

SCRABBLE

Ad Agency: MacLaren McCann Calgary, Canada | www.maclaren.com   **Client:** Randell's Drycleaning   **Title:** Nature's Favourite Drycleaner

Art Directors: Mike Meadus, Natalie Santucci   **Associate Creative Director:** Nicolle Pittman

Creative Director: Mike Meadus   **Photographer:** Justen Lacoursiere   **Copywriter:** Nicolle Pittman

ASSIGNMENT

Randell's is Calgary's first organic dry cleaner, offering chemical-free service to the busy downtown white-collar crowd. As well as communicating that Randell's offered organic dry cleaning, we needed to create demand for organic dry cleaning among an audience that had never heard of it.

APPROACH

Randell's new beltline location is a block away from three yoga studios and four Starbucks. Ads needed to appeal to the neighbourhood's hippie elite, turning them into both customers and brand advocates.

BIG IDEA

"Nature's Favourite Drycleaner" came first. From there we hit the local Devonian Gardens (sorry), four mall planters (sorry), and two flower shops to find exotic leaves that looked like ties. Simple, elegant photography let the props tell the story. Whose delicates are more delicate than Nature's?

RESULTS

As part of a poster series, this ad helped to position Randell's as the area's eco-conscious option. Visually demonstrating the benefit of organic dry cleaning gained us credibility in the minds of our audience and made them smile, which never hurts. Randell's neighborhood clientele is more loyal than ever.

Ad Agency: Publicis Dallas, USA | www.publicis-usa.com   **Client:** Terminix   **Title:** Crack

Art Director: Dustin Taylor   **Copywriter:** Andrew Beckman   **Creative Directors:** Julia Melle, Pete Voehringer, Steve Grimes

Executive Creative Director: Shon Rathbone   **Photographer:** Justin Clemmons   **Print Producer:** Katy Theiss

BRIEF

This Terminix Roach insert was created to support the current "Seeing is Believing" Terminix campaign which aims to convince homeowners they should be proactive versus reactive when it comes to their pest control. Homeowners typically see a bug, kill a bug. So for them to be proactive, we need to help them see what's lurking behind their walls and understand the real threat pests pose to their home.

SOLUTION

We created a disruptive way to help homeowners see what they usually can't see — pests entering their home through a very small crack. In this case, the center bind represented the small space it takes for pests to enter a home. And by placing the insert in the middle of a Dallas Home Tour brochure, we found a way to expose the truth in a powerfully relevant medium. As homeowners toured the beautiful homes, they felt the importance of "getting to pests, before pests get to them".

All it takes is a small crack for a cockroach to enter your home.

TERMINIX Power over pests.

Ad Agency: Publicis Dallas, USA | www.publicis-usa.com   **Client:** Terminix   **Title:** Sawdust House

Agency Producer: Jaime Roderer   **Art Director:** Dustin Taylor   **Copywriter:** Andrew Beckman

Creative Directors: Julia Melle, Pete Voehringer, Steve Grimes   **Executive Creative Director:** Shon Rathbone   **Photographer:** Scott Harben

BRIEF

This guerilla execution, Terminix Sawdust House, was created to support the current "Seeing is Believing" Terminix campaign which aims to convince homeowners they should be proactive versus reactive when it comes to their pest control. Homeowners typically see a bug, kill a bug. So for them to be proactive, we need to help them see what's lurking behind their walls and understand the real threat pests pose to their home.

SOLUTION

We created a disruptive way to help homeowners understand the amount of damage termites can do to their homes. A large pile of sawdust, placed on an empty lot in a suburban neighborhood, dramatizes the effect that termites can have on your home. It made homeowners understand the importance of "getting to pests, before pests get to them."

Ad Agency: TAXI CANADA INC, Calgary, Canada | www.taxi.ca   **Client:** Pak-N-Stor   **Title:** Box

Art Director: Kelsey Horne   **Creative Director:** Trent Burton   **Photographer:** Jason Stang   **Copywriter:** Nick Asik

ASSIGNMENT

The object was to position Pak-N-Stor as the place to store your stuff when your home no longer can.

APPROACH

Let's talk directly about the benefit of storing your possessions. But let's do it in a way that rewards the reader both in the headline and the visual presentation.

BIG IDEA

Let's build the headlines out of Storage Boxes and photograph them in situation. The use of white creates a sense of space and allows for the type to stand out.

RESULTS

The client is in love with the work and has seen a marked increase in business because of them.

Ad Agency: TAXI CANADA INC, Calgary, Canada | www.taxi.ca   **Client:** Hazco Demolition   **Title:** Blue Print

Account Director: Ginny Wetmore   **Art Director:** Kelsey Horne   **Creative Director:** Trent Burton

Illustrator: Replicate Designs   **Photographer:** Jason Stang   **Print Producer:** Marsha Walters   **Copywriter:** Nick Asik

ASSIGNMENT

How do you make HAZCO Demolition top of mind with architects and planners when they're ready to start a new project?

APPROACH

The challenge was that every architect and planner has a thorough understanding of what's involved with demolishing a building. With that being the case, we didn't need to educate them on the HAZCO process, but rather use creativity to make HAZCO their first choice.

BIG IDEA

Let's use their language to show them what HAZCO does. Using CAD software, we created an actual architectural blueprint of a HAZCO demolition site, printed it on architectural bond paper and sent it to potential customers in an architectural tube.

RESULTS

The client was extremely pleased with the results, and while the potential client base for their services is fairly small, feedback from architects and planners has been very positive.

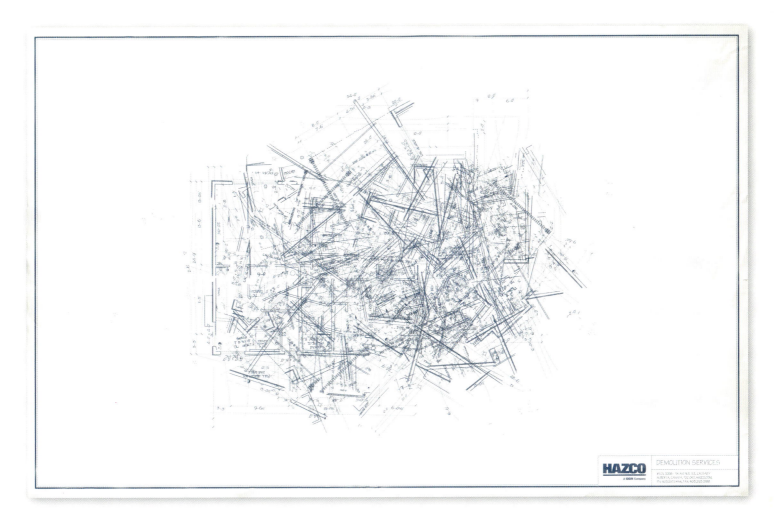

Ad Agency: O'Leary & Partners, Newport Beach, CA, USA | www.adagency.com   **Client:** AAA Mid-Atlantic   **Title:** Useful In Ways You Might Not Expect

Art Director: Paul Christensen   **Copywriter:** Matt McNelis   **Executive Creative Directors:** Eric Spiegler, Deidre McQuaide

AAA was losing relevance with consumers because of the perception that AAA's primary benefit is providing roadside assistance. Yet the benefits of being a AAA member are much greater than that. We were asked to develop a campaign that informs current and potential members of all the additional benefits (vacation planning, shopping/entertainment discounts and auto repair, to name a few) that come with membership.

We developed a campaign that literally puts giant AAA cards in environments where members might enjoy discounts and services. A wide variety of executions were used to showcase the AAA card as a symbolic representation of the benefits delivered by AAA or the member. A simple line of copy asks people to "Use it for all it's worth."

Membership is on the rise, and research shows that awareness for AAA product/service categories outside of Roadside Assistance has gone from low to moderately high — with a 30% increase in travel services awareness, and 56% awareness in shopping discounts.

Sports packages. AAA. Use it for all it's worth.® **AAA.com**

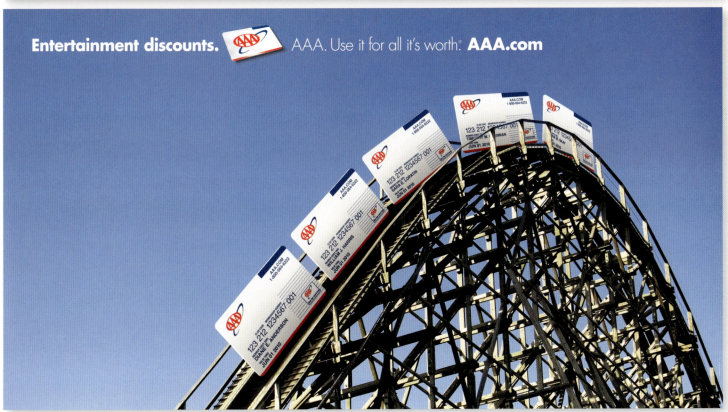

Entertainment discounts. AAA. Use it for all it's worth.® **AAA.com**

Ad Agency: Lindsay, Stone & Briggs, Madison, WI, USA | www.lsb.com   **Client:** The Psychic Gallery   **Title:** Psychic Gallery Point of Purchase

Art Director: Matt Johanning   **Copywriter:** Lee Schmidt

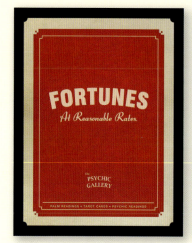 

The Psychic Gallery, a storefront business, offers tarot card readings and palm readings. Research showed that some people are put off by the prospect of seeing a fortune teller. They view it as ominous. "Will I be dealt the 'death card?'" "Do I have a short life line?" These point-of-sale materials use humor to create a lighter attitude about visiting the Psychic Gallery. They encourage people to see The Psychic Gallery as a fun place where having a fortune told is entertaining, not scary.

Welcome.

WE'VE BEEN

expecting you.

The
PSYCHIC
GALLERY

PALM READINGS • TAROT CARDS • PSYCHIC READINGS

Ad Agency: Heller Communication Design, Brooklyn, NY, USA | www.hellercd.com   **Client:** Creative Edge Parties   **Title:** Creative Edge Parties Campaign   **Art Director:** Cheryl Heller   **Designer:** Sarah Seybert

About six years ago, we developed an identity for Creative Edge Parties using an egg as a symbol of creativity, ideas and versatility. Based on that identity, we developed a print advertising campaign for them that featured fancy chickens. It worked. Their business grew significantly. It was memorable and people loved it.

This ad, with the cow who has laid a perfect egg, is the first in a new campaign evolving the identity and committing to the impossible.

Ad Agency: TBWA\PHS Helsinki, Finland | www.tbwa.fi   **Client:** Young Director Award by CFP-E/Shots   **Title:** Pool

Art Director: Minna Lavola   **Copywriters:** Mira Olsson, Markku Haapalehto   **Designers:** Margit Mardisalu, Sanna Tamminen

Illustrator: Fake Graphics   **Photographer:** Jere Hietala   **Project Manager:** Kirsi Parni

OBJECTIVE

Create awareness for the Young Director Award by CFP-E/Shots.

CONCEPT

Directors are born, not made. We show a little boy being a natural born director and bringing some drama into his everyday.

TARGET AUDIENCE

Commercial production professionals and young directors.

Ad Agency: TAXI CANADA INC, Calgary, Canada | www.taxi.ca   **Client:** Gold's Gym   **Title:** Truck Lift, Kate's Couch

Account Director: Gord Ellis   **Art Director:** Kelsey Horne

Creative Director: Trent Burton   **Photographer:** Justen Lacoursiere   **Print Producer:** Marsha Walters   **Copywriter:** Nick Asik

ASSIGNMENT

Raise awareness of how a membership at Gold's Gym can help you become the "man you want to be".

APPROACH

The challenge here was to show the benefit of working out, while avoiding the hackneyed "meatheads lifting heavy stuff" visuals you so often see. People know the benefits of joining a gym. We wanted to show that in a different and fresh way.

BIG IDEA

Show "gym members" engaged in exaggerated activities that they'd never be able to complete if not for their membership at Gold's. We used exaggeration, but not in an obvious way. The viewer takes a moment or two before they realize what they're looking at.

RESULTS

The client was very happy with the work and has had excellent feedback from potential members.

Ad Agency: Goodby, Silverstein & Partners, San Francisco, USA | www.gspsf.com   **Client:** Hewlett Packard   **Title:** Go Green Airplane

Art Director: Andre Massis   **Creative Director:** Will McGinness   **Photographer:** Claude Shade   **Copywriter:** Jordan Kramer

The HP "Go Green Airplane" poster was created to highlight the lengths to which HP has gone to reduce e-waste. The use of thousands of discarded computers, photographed in an HP technology recycling plant, creates the outline of a jumbo jet and highlights the fact that the company has recycled the equivalent weight of 1,200 such airplanes to date.

WE FIGURE IF YOU'RE GOING TO RECYCLE, GO BIG.

Since 1987, HP has collected
a billion pounds of e-waste –
the weight of 1,200 jumbo jets.
Visit hp.com/go/consumerbuyback
to find out how you can help
HP recover, refurbish, and recycle
2 billion pounds of e-waste
by the end of 2010.

Ad Agency: Martin|Williams, Minneapolis, USA | www.martinwilliams.com   **Client:** Boy Scouts of America   **Title:** Letter to the Editor

Art Director: Toby Balai   **Chief Creative Officer:** Tom Moudry   **Copywriter:** Adam Ridgeway   **Creative Director:** Jeff Tresidder

Since it's inception in 1910, the Boys Scouts of America have held true to their "BE PREPARED" motto. For the BSA's one-hundredth anniversary, Martin|Williams was challenged with showing just how fundamental this belief is to the organization. Rather than just saying, "Scouts are prepared," we thought it would be more appropriate to demonstrate it. The resulting newspaper ad uses a feeling of history to show there's nothing Boy Scouts aren't prepared for, even an anniversary that's 100 years away.

THE BOY SCOUTS OF AMERICA
HENNEPIN COUNCIL

February 8th, 1910

Dear Editor,

Enclosed is the artwork for our upcoming
Boy Scouts of America centennial advertisement.
Please place and run in your publication in
100 years.

Sincerely yours,

W.F. Webster

W.F. Webster
Council President,
Boy Scouts of America

BE PREPARED.

BOY SCOUTS OF AMERICA
Celebrating 100 years of Scouting.

Ad Agency: Lewis Communications, Birmingham, AL, USA | www.lewiscommunications.com   **Client:** Habitat For Humanity   **Title:** Habitat For Humanity Ad Campaign
Account Directors: Larry Norris, Miriam Strickland, Roy Burns   **Art Directors:** Jason Bickell, Spencer Till   **Associate Creative Director:** Roy Burns
Copywriters: Mike Brady, Stephen Curry, Spencer Till   **Creative Director:** Stephen Curry   **Executive Creative Director:** Spencer Till
Photographer: Jeff Williams   **Photographer's Assistant:** Benjamin Fine   **Print Producers:** Benjamin Fine, Leigh Ann Motley

Habitat For Humanity is an enormously respected charity. But the brand also comes with a lot of built-in perceptions. Before we started, we looked at work that had been done for other chapters around the country.

So much of it seemed to employ the usual tugging-on-heartstrings with smiling people and hammers and a message about the joy of the sweat of your brow.

In truth, what the organization really needed more than anything else was additional financial support.

We wanted to speak to people in a more authentic way, breaking through traditional expectations of what it means to help Habitat, and convince them that we're all in a position to make a difference — even those of us not particularly adept with tools.

1142

61-1/620

DATE Nov 10, 2009

$

DOLLARS

Your donation can make all the difference.

Habitat
for Humanity®
Greater Birmingham

habitatbirmingham.org/donate

Ad Agency: Pyper Paul + Kenney, Tampa, FL, USA | www.pyperpaul.com   **Client:** ASPCA   **Title:** Speechless Dog

Account Director: Jesse Vahsholtz   **Art Director:** Aaron Riney   **Associate Creative Director:** Michael Schillig

Copywriter: Michael Schillig   **Executive Creative Director:** Tom Kenney

This was a poster designed to make people aware of the ASPCA (The American Society for the Prevention of Cruelty to Animals) and encourage them to be a voice for abused animals. We wanted to reinforce the ASPCA's existing theme line, "We Are Their Voice," and illustrate in the most simple, emotionally powerful way how animals cannot speak out against cruelty and must rely on us to do that for them.

ANIMALS CAN'T SPEAK OUT AGAINST CRUELTY. BUT YOU CAN.

ASPCA®
ASPCA.ORG
WE ARE THEIR VOICE®

Ad Agency: bvk, Milwaukee, WI, USA | www.bvk.com **Client:** City of Milwaukee County Health Department **Title:** What Did You Touch Today?

Art Director: Rich Kohnke **Creative Directors:** Gary Mueller, Rich Kohnke **Digital Artist/Multimedia:** Jim McDonald **Photographer:** Nick Collura **Copywriter:** Mike Holicek

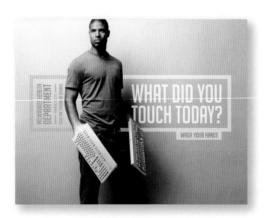

With the arrival of the H1-N1 virus and seasonal flu, a national effort to educate the public on prevention has gained urgency. Partnering with Serve and 14 local public health agencies, the City of Milwaukee Health Department joined the cause with a regional multimedia campaign in 2009. Outdoor and bus shelter executions were designed to raise awareness of the everyday mundane situations that present risks for the spreading of flu viruses. To stand out, and connect with a younger audience that may not think twice about the things they touch in a typical day, the ads present fashionably photographed people whose arms have literally (and oddly) become the objects they touch. Broadcast and other media promoted good hygiene practices and vaccination.

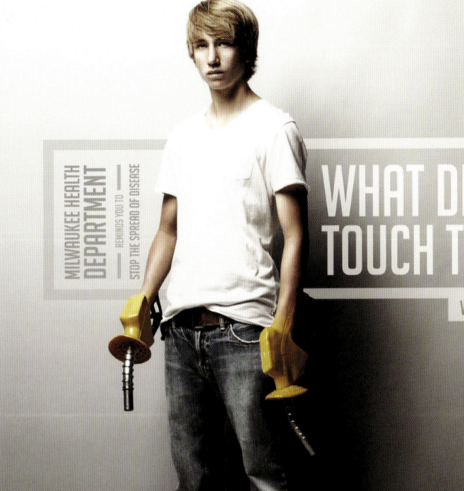

Ad Agency: Laughlin Constable, Milwaukee, WI, USA | www.laughlin.com   **Client:** Red Cross   **Title:** Calm After The Storm

Art Director: Michael Vojvodich   **Copywriter:** David Hanneken   **Creative Director:** David Hanneken   **Digital Artists/Multimedia:** Gina Ferrise, Chris Metcalf

This ad was designed to draw attention to the Red Cross' capabilities to assist in the aftermath of a storm. For many, the Red Cross is known as an organization that organizes blood drives and meal programs. Since Hurricane Katrina, they have raised their profile and this ad was designed to help care that momentum forward.

By utilizing dramatic photography of a rusty, weathered chain-link fence we wanted this image to feel as it was in the thick of the storm. The water in the background provides a sense that the floodwaters have subsided and all that is left is our good name. The call-to-action, while not primary to the message of awareness, still in its own way asked the audience to volunteer or donate much needed funds.

Ad Agency: bvk, Milwaukee, WI, USA | www.bvk.com   **Client:** City Of Milwaukee County Health Department   **Title:** Headstone

Art Directors: Mike Scalise, Cheryl Peaslee   **Creative Director:** Gary Mueller   **Digital Artist/Multimedia:** Jim McDonald   **Photographer:** Jim McDonald   **Copywriter:** Mike Holicek

Facing an unacceptable number of infant deaths in Milwaukee every year, the City of Milwaukee Health Department wanted to raise awareness of the risks of sharing a bed with a baby, commonly referred to as "co-sleeping." This issue has become a lightning rod in many communities where parents defend the practice as a perfectly safe way of bonding with their newborn babies.

The direct, hard-hitting campaign was careful not to tell parents to stop sleeping with their babies, but to educate them about the suffocation and rollover risks — making it clear that the safest place for a baby to sleep is in a crib. The campaign has led to significant local media coverage and sparked continuing debate among parents, health officials and community leaders alike.

FOR TOO MANY BABIES LAST YEAR, THIS WAS THEIR FINAL RESTING PLACE.

Think twice before sleeping with your baby.
The safest place is in a crib.

City of Milwaukee Health Department · www.milwaukee.com/safesleep

Ad Agency: Laughlin Constable, Milwaukee, WI, USA | www.laughlin.com   **Client:** Ronald McDonald House   **Title:** Heart, Shoes

Art Director: Chad Nauta   **Creative Director:** David Hanneken   **Digital Artists/Multimedia:** Gina Ferrise, Chris Metcalf   **Photographer:** Jeff Salzer

The Ronald McDonald House provides cash-strapped families with a place to stay, free of charge, while their child is recovering from complications due to cancer. To build awareness to this cause, we wanted to elicit emotion by marrying two images into one. Specifically, a photograph of a child integrated into a photograph of Ronald McDonald. We made the decision early on to not show Ronald's face or even most of his body, but rather showcase subtle hints of his participation in the family's emotional battle. Ronald is there for the child. He is there for the family. He cares for kids. And it is his support (in essence, the McDonald's Corporation) that ensures families are in good hands. The Ronald McDonald House does not help to cure cancer, but they do provide families who are strapped for cash with one less thing to worry about when it comes to where they stay and where to eat.

RONALD
McDONALD
HOUSE

© 2009 McDonald's

RONALD
McDONALD
HOUSE

© 2009 McDonald's

Ad Agency: Clarity Coverdale Fury, Minneapolis, USA | www.ccf-ideas.com   Client: Mothers Against Drunk Driving   Title: Don't Be A Model For Binge Drinking

Art Director: Karl Madcharo   Copywriter: Michael Atkinson   Creative Director: Jac Coverdale   Photographer: William Clark

Motivate college students to discuss the realities of binge drinking. Applications: Designed to be flexible posting units — handouts, dorms, student events and campus buildings.

FORMAL WEAR
BY BINGE

THE MAJORITY OF PEOPLE WHO DIE FROM ALCOHOL POISONING RECEIVE NO HELP FROM THEIR FRIENDS. DON'T BE A MODEL FOR BINGE DRINKING. UMADD

BEAUTY
BY BINGE

71% OF COLLEGE WOMEN BELIEVE MEN FIND IT ATTRACTIVE WHEN THEY DRINK MORE. DON'T BE A MODEL FOR BINGE DRINKING. UMADD

Ad Agency: Pyper Paul + Kenney, Tampa, FL, USA | www.pyperpaul.com   **Client:** Metropolitan Ministries   **Title:** Doll

Art Director: Ben Day   **Associate Creative Director:** Joey Crawford   **Executive Creative Director:** Tom Kenney   **Photographer:** Ben Day

Our client, Metropolitan Ministries, does amazing things for the region, so anytime we do work with them, we want to make sure the work is equally amazing. But being a non-profit client, we have to do the amazing, but also amazing on the cheap. So when they came to us to do a campaign to create awareness for their deep need of toys during the holiday season, we knew it would be a challenge, especially with the added pressure of having the Christmases of thousands and thousands of kids in our hands. Metropolitan Ministries is the only way they are able to get toys. So, if there aren't enough toys, there isn't Christmas for theses children in need. A harrowing thought.

When we were concepting this series of ads, we kept coming back to the idea that toys aren't just toys, they are vessels of hope, comfort and love. Sure, it's just a piece of manufactured plastic, but for kids who have nothing, it shows them that someone cares, that there is a reason to hope. So, we wanted to show toys that literally care. And we had just watched Toy Story, which inspired the anthroporphization of the toys.

In terms of budget, there was none. The art director was the photographer. Another art director was the arm model (she has very young looking arms). The doll we bought, but then donated to Metropolitan Ministries.

Ad Agency: bvk, Milwaukee, WI, USA | www.bvk.com   **Client:** United Way   **Title:** Scratch and Sniff
Art Directors: GiHo Lee, Ben Halpin   **Creative Director:** Gary Mueller   **Copywriter:** Gary Mueller

This fake interactive bus shelter is part of a three-year community effort to deglamorize teen pregnancy in Milwaukee (Milwaukee recently had the 2nd highest rate of births to teens in the country).

The dirty diaper bus shelters dared students waiting for the bus on the first day back at school to see if it was really a scratch and sniff poster. Upon closer inspection however, they saw a message inside the scratch and sniff dot that read, "This ad doesn't really stink, but the consequences of teen pregnancy sure do."

The bus shelter caused a stir among students and the media resulting in dozens of media stories and hundreds of blog posts online. The multi-campaign effort is being credited with a 10% drop in teen pregnancy in the City of Milwaukee — the largest drop in 30 years.

SCRATCH AND SNIFF

This doesn't really smell.
But the consequences of teen pregnancy sure do.
And this is just part of the ugly mess you'd be getting
yourself into. Get the facts at scratchansniff.com.

Ad Agency: 22squared, Tampa, FL, USA | www.22squared.com　　**Client:** Partnership For A Drug-Free America　　**Title:** Bong, Paint Can, Pill Bottle

Art Director: Derek Kirkman　　**Copywriter:** Kevin Botfeld　　**Creative Director:** John Stapleton

ASSIGNMENT

To promote drugfree.org, The Partnership For A Drugfree America asked us to create a campaign aimed at providing parents tools, tips and knowledge to intervene with your child if they suspect drug use.

APPROACH

All production and media was donated. Therefore, the challenge was to create a simple, provocative and effective idea. And urge parents to log onto drugfree.org for expert advice, helpful tips, in-depth stories and to connect with other parents in the same situation.

THE BIG IDEA

Having a serious talk with your kids about drugs is never easy. As part of a multi-media campaign, these ads prompt parents to think about how they would handle a tough situation. Although there is no right answer, there is a place where you can find out how to better answer them.

what would you say?
learn at drugfree.org

Ad Agency: Euro RSCG Chicago, USA | www.eurorscg.com   Client: Newcity   Title: "Unassimilate" Campaign

Art Directors: Matt Dimmer, Jason Tisser   Copywriter: Regan Kline   Chief Creative Director: Blake Ebel

Our objective was to tout Newcity's reputation as a free-thinking alternative press outlet, and encourage readership for this unique paper amidst a sea of homogeneous media sources. The "Unassimilate" campaign targets educated, well-read Chicagoans, and implores them to stop being spoon-fed their information and to discover a smarter source that is unique to both their city and themselves. The client was thrilled by the arresting visuals and fervent call-to-action copy, and ran the ads in and around Chicago as both print and posters.

REJECT THE HERD MENTALITY.   UNASSIMILATE.

NEWCITY

Ad Agency: DeVito/Verdi, New York, USA | www.devitoverdi.com   **Client:** Legal Sea Foods   **Title:** Porthole

Art Director: Zack Menna   **Copywriter:** Bonnie Pihl   **Creative Director:** Sal DeVito

Legal Sea Foods has one clear, consistent point of difference — the freshness/quality of their fish. With such a simple strategy, against which we have executed for a number of years, the agency's challenge is to consistently develop fresh ways to communicate such a straightforward message. When creating this concept we wanted to keep the visual simple and eye catching. By combining two very familiar images, a place setting and a porthole, we hoped to create something visually interesting. It was also important to keep the visual appetizing, since we were advertising for a restaurant. Therefore, we chose a very clean, ascetically pleasing shot of the ocean. We hoped that the viewer would take away a sense that when sitting down for a meal at Legal Sea Foods they should expect the seafood to be as ocean fresh as humanly possible.

legalseafoods.com

Ad Agency: Concussion LLP, Fort Worth, TX, USA | www.concussion.net   **Client:** Shooting Star Casino   **Title:** Mustang Lounge Posters   **Chief Creative Officer:** Andrew Yanez

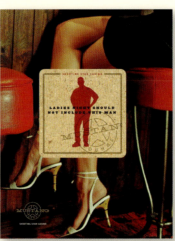

CASE STUDY: NEW IDENTITY DEVELOPMENT AND BRANDING

While mostly known for endless lakes and beautiful farming land, Mahnomen, Minnesota, home of Shooting Star Casino, is a key attraction for residents of Fargo, North Dakota, Northwest Minnesota and Southern Manitoba. With a sizeable casino, hotel, spa and events center, the property has long been the top casino draw for the region, representing a significant revenue enterprise for the White Earth Nation.

ASSIGNMENT

Shooting Star has traditionally targeted older, more mature gamblers with its branding messages. As more competitors began to follow Shooting Star's lead, the strategy became commoditized, diluting its efficacy in distinguishing Shooting Star from its competitive set. In order to attract a younger customer base, Shooting Star added new amenities to appeal to a new generation of gamers. Among those amenities was the renovation of the Mustang Lounge, designed to mimic the feel of a Las Vegas nightclub, with mood lighting, a dramatic stage and round cocktail seating. Concussion was charged with developing a new identity for Mustang Lounge that would resonate with a younger demographic while tapping into a key emotional state — the desire for a hipper nightlife experience than what was currently available in the region.

THE BIG IDEA

In developing a new identity for the Mustang Lounge, it was essential that we connect with Shooting Star's brand essence — "Come Out and Shine." The Mustang Lounge offered the opportunity for younger customers to come out to "see and be seen" in a hip nightclub environment — their chance to "Shine" while socializing, dancing, enjoying live music and partaking in their favorite beverages. Concussion determined that an iconic approach was essential to communicate the Mustang Lounge experience and reposition that experience in the mind of consumers. And what could be a more iconic representation of the nightclub experience than a bar coaster? The new identity and branding featured a bar coaster with headlines conveying that the Mustang Lounge was not a typical bar experience. This message was supported with imagery of young men and women, along with the all-important beverages, to contemporize the brand and infuse a sense of fun and entertainment. In doing so, perceptions of the Mustang Lounge as a tired bar were transformed into thoughts of a wild ride in the hottest nightclub in the region.

RESULTS

Both traffic and beverage revenue enjoyed double-digit increases in the first three months following the renovation and launch of the new brand campaign. Traffic and revenue levels continue to be sustained, consistently exceeding same period prior year levels while also drawing the younger customer base that is essential for Shooting Star's long-term viability in the marketplace.

SHOOTING STAR CASINO
GET THE COLD SHOULDER,
THEN A COLD DRINK
MUSTANG
MUSTANG
LOUNGE
SHOOTING STAR CASINO

Ad Agency: Bill Santry Design, Arlington, VA, USA | www.billsantrydesign.com

Art Director: Bill Santry

Client: 3 Bar and Grill

Copywriter: Aaron Spratt

Title: Fill-In-The-Blank Napkins

Creative Director: Bill Santry

ASSIGNMENT

We needed to draw attention to 3 Bar and Grill as a Valentine's Day destination in the crowded metro DC bar scene.

APPROACH

Arlington has a large population of young professional singles. We took advantage of this by creating something bar patrons could actually use and would enjoy passing along to others.

THE BIG IDEA

"Hookup facilitation devices" — specially branded cocktail napkins people could use to share their contact information, while serving as a reminder of the good time they had at 3 Bar and Grill.

RESULTS

The napkins were a big hit, generating lots of word of mouth, blog mentions and press for the restaurant. The client continues to use the napkins today, long after the Valentine's Day promotion ended, and even keeps some of the funnier customer submissions on file.

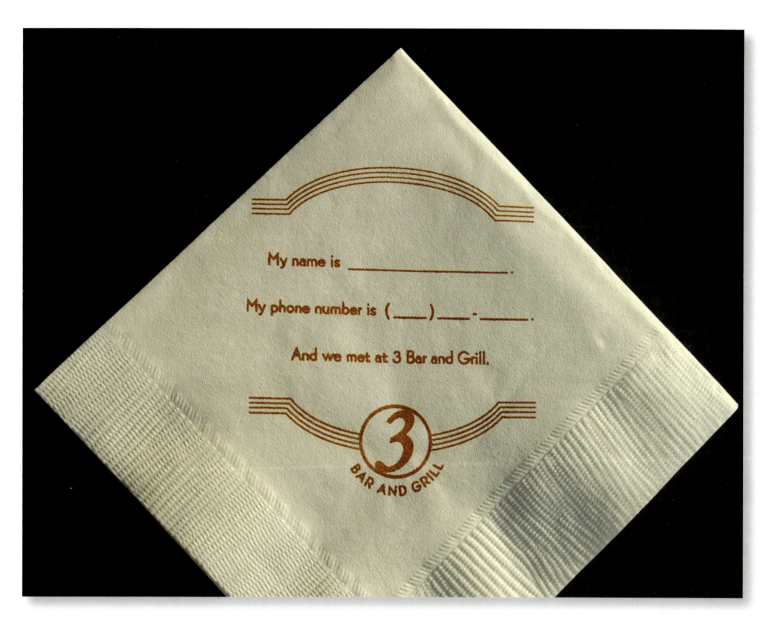

Ad Agency: Duncan/Channon, San Francisco, USA | www.duncanchannon.com   **Client:** Sanita Clogs, Inc   **Title:** Sanita: The Original Danish Clog

Copywriter: Parker Channon   **Creative Director:** Anne Elisco-Lemme   **Digital Artist/Multimedia:** Jennifer Moe

Photographer: Morten Bengstsson   **Print Producer:** Jacqueline Fodor

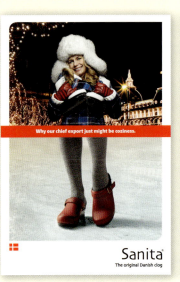

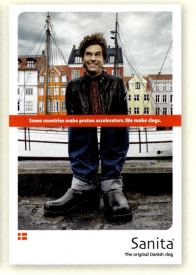

Hygge. It's a Danish word meaning to make everything cozy and comfortable — and the basis of this campaign for Denmark's original clog company, Sanita. Emphasizing a century of Danish craftsmanship speaks to Sanita's quality and differentiates them from their chief competitor Dansko, who manufactures their clogs in China.

Clogs. 50 million Danish toes can't be wrong.

Sanita®

The original Danish clog

Ad Agency: Davidson Branding, Richmond, VA, USA | www.davidsonbranding.com   **Client:** Secrets Shhh   **Title:** Flowers   **Project Manager:** Tammy Morgan

Flowers have become a metaphor for the beauty, simplicity and style associated with Secrets Shhh simulated diamonds. This new and iconic imagery sets Secrets Shhh apart from their competitors.

These advertisements are run in numerous magazines throughout Australia that target confident, self assured, stylish and fashion conscious females who value and appreciate beauty.

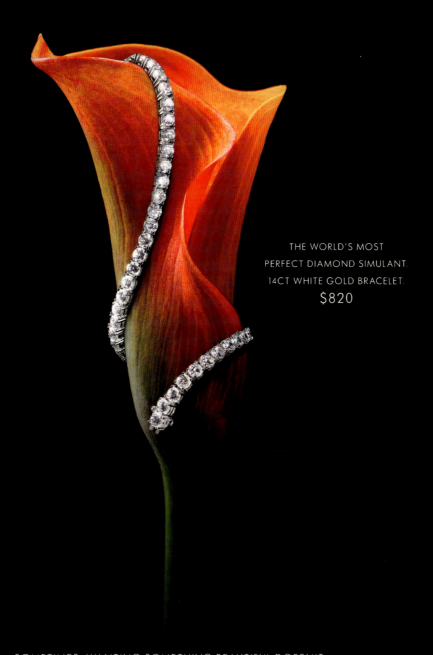

THE WORLD'S MOST
PERFECT DIAMOND SIMULANT.
14CT WHITE GOLD BRACELET.
$820

SOMETIMES, WANTING SOMETHING BEAUTIFUL DOESN'T
NEED TO BE JUSTIFIED OR EXPLAINED.
HOW IT MAKES YOU FEEL IS REASON ENOUGH.

SYDNEY MELBOURNE BRISBANE ADELAIDE PERTH NEWCASTLE GOLD COAST CAIRNS NOOSA AUCKLAND.
WWW.SECRETS-SHHH.COM

Ad Agency: TBWA\PHS Helsinki, Finland | www.tbwa.fi   **Client:** Instrumentarium   **Title:** Picasso, Matisse   **Account Director:** Eija Anteroinen   **Art Directors:** Mikko Torvinen, Ossi Honkanen

Copywriters: Erkko Mannila, Tommy Makinen, Antti Toivonen   **Creative Director:** Mikko Torvinen   **Illustrator:** Tommi Vallisto   **Project Managers:** Karolina Mattsson, Kirsi Parni

ASSIGNMENT

Optician Instrumentarium is an expert in Finnish eyesight and vision with a 100-year history. Instrumentarium wanted to retain its strong position as an expert and top quality and combine stylish advertising to them. It also wanted to inform people of the affections of aging to the eyesight.

APPROACH

We decided to strengthen the association between eye-glasses and high intelligence and communicate the affections of aging to the eyesight in a stylish way, but with a tint of humour.

THE BIG IDEA

Our big idea was that everybody's eyesight weakens when getting older, even those with the sharpest vision, even the most unique individuals of us. We made print ads that show several paintings of two famous painters, Pablo Picasso and Henri Matisse from their different periods. It's generally known that both developed their style from realistic paintings to the very stylized ones.

RESULTS

The ads awakened positive attention and feedback. Instrumentarium strengthened its strong position as a leading optician in Finland with a stylish and memorable way and attracted new customers.

1907

1917

1927

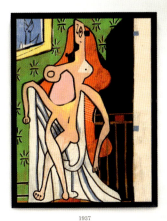

1937

Buy eye-glasses before it's too late.

1919

1939

1947

1952

Buy eye-glasses before it's too late.

Ad Agency: Factory Design Labs, Denver, USA | www.factorylabs.com   **Client:** Revo   **Title:** Look Deeper   **Account Director:** Kam Rope

Artist: Stephen Hausrath   **Copywriter:** Mike King   **Creative Director:** Josh Wills   **Executive Creative Director:** Steve Whittier   **Photographer:** Richard Schultz

BRAND RE-LAUNCH CAMPAIGN

In the 1980s, Revo was the polarized sunglasses brand of the day. However, as the rise of polarized sunglasses took hold, Revo started to lose its unique brand presence as well as its market share. In 2008, eyewear giant Luxottica acquired Revo and called on Factory to re-launch the brand in support of a completely new product line.

CHALLENGE

We were tasked with repositioning and reintroducing the Revo brand into the marketplace as the leader in polarized lens technology. At the same time, we needed to stay relevant to the brand's key demographic: Outdoor enthusiasts.

SOLUTION

We took the Revo brand and completely reinvented it with an integrated campaign titled "Look Deeper," a story rooted in technology, adventure and the environment. We introduced the idea of outdoor adventurers Jimmy Chin and Alexandra Cousteau as the faces of Revo while telling a story of sustainability and superior polarization technology. Alongside a major in-store and point-of-purchase presence, the campaign includes print, collateral and the completely redesigned Revo.com.

RESULTS

As of August 2009, Revo tripled its presence within primary retail outlets. Overall brand sales have exceeded all projected goals to date, and the success of the Sunglass Hut front door campaign many stores opted to keep Revo marketing for additional weeks.

LOOK DEEPER™

ALEXANDRA COUSTEAU

GLOBAL WATER ADVOCATE.
GROWING UP AMONGST THE OCEAN, ALEXANDRA COUSTEAU EXPERIENCED THE POWER OF CONSERVATION FIRSTHAND. TODAY, HER FAMILY'S LEGACY LIVES ON IN A JOURNEY TO BELIZE. IN THE COUNTRY HER GRANDFATHER EXPLORED OVER 30 YEARS AGO, ALEXANDRA CONTINUES HER MISSION OF DOCUMENTING THE ISSUES FACING OUR GLOBAL WATER SYSTEM AND EDUCATING PEOPLE ON THE IMPORTANCE OF PROTECTING IT.

ALEXANDRA WEARING THE REVO WAYPOINT IN BELIZE

LOOK DEEPER™

JIMMY CHIN

CLIMBER. SKIER. PHOTOGRAPHER. EXPLORER.
JIMMY CHIN'S PASSION FOR EXPLORATION BEGAN IN JOSHUA TREE, CALIFORNIA. SURROUNDED BY THE UNIQUE LANDSCAPE JIMMY SPENT DAYS ON THE CRAG AND NIGHTS SLEEPING IN HIS CAR. AND WHILE THE DAYS OF SLEEPING IN HIS CAR ARE BEHIND HIM, HE CONTINUES TO APPROACH THE SPORT WITH THE SAME SENSE OF HUMILITY.

JIMMY WEARING THE REVO WAYPOINT IN JOSHUA TREE, CALIFORNIA

Ad Agency: Bussolati Associates, Washington, DC, USA | www.bussolati.com   **Client:** Bussolati   **Title:** Bussolati designs magazines

Creative Director: Monica Bussolati   **Designer:** Monica Bussolati

  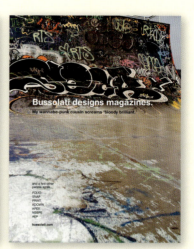

ASSIGNMENT

Bussolati is a studio with a core competency in publication design. Signature magazine, with its targeted readership of editorial teams, was identified as ideal for an ad campaign for our studio.

APPROACH

Many of the ads in this publication use images of magazine covers to show the advertiser's breadth of experience, but a reader flipping through the book can't easily glean which services the advertiser provides — design, ad sales or printing, etc. Our goal was to create an ad that clearly and quickly communicated that Bussolati 'designs' magazines.

THE BIG IDEA

At one point in our creative process, we actually heard what we kept repeating — the ad should say 'Bussolati designs magazine.' So that became the headline and we added a comical subhead that would change for each placement. The studio owner's mother regularly comments that our work is "pretty," despite our explanation that while some of it may indeed be pretty, we are actually striving for effective a lot more than 'pretty.' Our first ad in the series read: Bussolati designs magazines. My mother says they're pretty. This campaign has a lot of legs; for years we have evolved the subhead copy and the visuals to keep it fresh for the readers and in sync with the publication issue's theme. We evolved the look from having a flat background color to using a background image — another opportunity for comic relief.

RESULTS

After the first placement, we received a few e-mails from readers who appreciated the ad. When we attend the annual conference of Signature's publisher, attendees stop by our booth and we enjoy easy conversation comparing which subheads we liked the best (Our accountant says they're number 1; My baker friend thinks they're sweet). Readers say they like the ads and — most importantly — they remember us because of the ads. We have been told that our ad campaign is how Bussolati was identified to be considered for their publication's design services.

Bussolati designs magazines.
Aunt Nikki likes them almost as much as shopping.

and a few other
people agree

FOLIO:
SNAP
PRINT
ADCMW
APEX
NSBPE
AEP

bussolati.com

Ad Agency: Erickson Productions, Inc., Petaluma, CA, USA | www.ericksonstock.com   **Client:** Erickson Stock   **Title:** Erickson Stock Advertisement Series
Designer: Nicki Krinsky   **Photographer:** Jim Erickson

ASSIGNMENT

Self-Promotional ads for Erickson Stock and Jim Erickson Assignment Photography

APPROACH

Behind the scenes photos were used to reveal the unique creative spirit of Jim and his crew

THE BIG IDEA

Erickson brand images are more than just a click of the camera. By showcasing the actual journey of producing an image library, potential clients are given an unexpected insight into what makes Erickson images stand apart from the rest.

RESULT

The six month campaign coincided with an overall increase in stock and assignment requests for early 2010.

Ad Agency: Goodby, Silverstein & Partners, San Francisco, USA | www.gspsf.com   **Client:** NBA   **Title:** Evolution

Art Director: Matt Ryan   **Creative Directors:** Jamie Barrett, Stefan Copiz, Ari Weiss   **Print Producer:** Suzee Barrabee   **Copywriter:** Ari Weiss

Every year the NBA playoffs crowns a new champion and creates a batch of new memories. That new champion, and those new memories are now permanently part of NBA history. In a sense, the NBA Playoffs connects to the past, present and future. With this execution we visually represent that thought. The great moments from Bill Russell to Magic Johnson to Michael Jordan to Kevin Garnett are all part of the same legacy and share one thing. They're champions.

Ad Agency: Mangos, Malvern, PA, USA | www.mangosinc.com   **Client:** Cannondale Bicycle Corporation   **Title:** Lefty Ad

Art Director: Derek Miller   **Associate Creative Directors:** Justin Moll, Charles Smolover   **Creative Director:** Joanne de Menna

Executive Creative Director: Bradley Gast   **Photographer:** Michael Furman   **Print Producer:** Lauren Nunnelee   **Project Manager:** Jeff Olivo

ASSIGNMENT

Cannondale is a bicycle builder with a cult-like brand that had lost touch with its following. So, it was time to take off the gloves and remind the world that Cannondale has never let anything stop it from engineering the ultimate cycling experience. That Cannondale has always fought to be different, not for the sake of being different, but for the sake of being the best.

APPROACH

The key challenge was to tell that story in a memorable way that avoided the clichés of typical bicycle advertising and clearly expressed Cannondale's unique positioning.

THE BIG IDEA

Mangos' solution was to create "The Good Fight," a gritty, global campaign created in 2009 that epitomized Cannondale's independent spirit. This ad for Cannondale's legendary Lefty 130mm PBR fork was part of that campaign and captured the feeling we were trying to convey.

RESULTS

The result was an unqualified victory. According to the 2009 Road Bike Action reader's survey, Cannondale went from fourth place to first as the brand of road bike most riders planned to buy next.

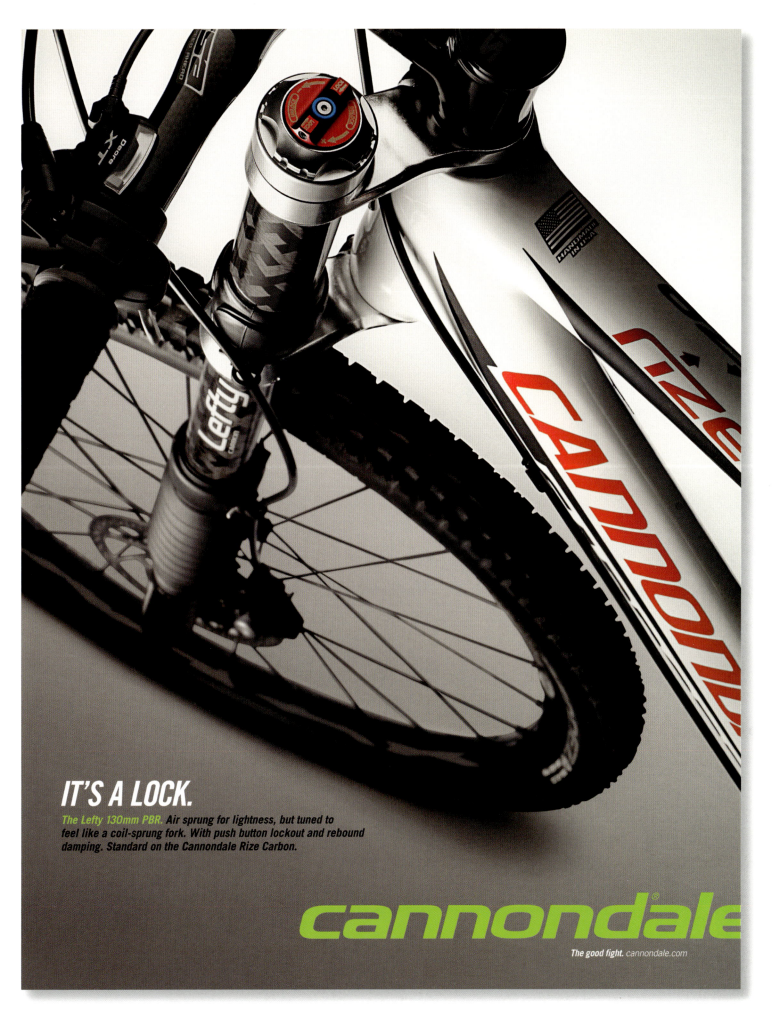

IT'S A LOCK.

The Lefty 130mm PBR. Air sprung for lightness, but tuned to
feel like a coil-sprung fork. With push button lockout and rebound
damping. Standard on the Cannondale Rize Carbon.

cannondale

The good fight. cannondale.com

Ad Agency: The Martin Agency, Richmond, VA, USA | www.martinagency.com   Client: NASCAR   Title: Engineering

Art Director: Randall Hooker   Creative Director: Cliff Sorah   Copywriter: Mark Billows

The NASCAR Nationwide Series is where drivers develop their skills to hopefully one day compete in the Sprint Cup Series — much like the minor leagues is to Major League Baseball. We felt that this aspect of seeing raw talent learn the ropes of racing was the real draw to the excitement of the sport. So, we decided to highlight this developmental process that takes place for drivers. We also wanted every ad to visually represent learning and racing, and that led us to having our ads drawn on asphalt with chalk as if it were a blackboard. An interesting characteristic of the Nationwide Series is that many of the big time Sprint Cup drivers often choose to race in this series. This makes for an interesting learning dynamic, which we try to convey in the Professor–Student execution.

STUDENT STUDENT STUDENT STUDENT STUDENT STUDENT

PROFESSOR

Where drivers get schooled.

Ad Agency: DeVito/Verdi, New York, USA | www.devitoverdi.com   **Client:** E.P. Carillo Cigars   **Title:** Dictators

Art Director: Manny Santos   **Copywriter:** Eric Schutte   **Creative Director:** Sal DeVito

Ernesto Perez-Carrillo, a world famous cigar maker, came out of retirement to create a new cigar company. He has made cigars for celebrities, presidents and even dictators. The assignment was to announce Ernesto's coming out of retirement, and that he's introducing his new line of cigars made from three different tobacco leaves from three different countries: Nicaragua, Dominican Republic and Ecuador. It is absolutely one of the finest cigars ever made. Special, inaugural edition cigars were made to commemorate his new cigar company. Only a limited supply of these fine cigars was available, and to cigar aficionados, news of Ernesto's new cigar is comparable to Mac introducing the first iPod. The whole world was waiting for it. Buyers and sellers alike lined up in cigar conventions trying to get the first look at Ernesto's new cigar. But only a few will get them. The ad is supposed to generate excitement and awareness throughout the cigar world. It was run in cigar magazines like Cigar Aficionado. It told the world that the cigar maker everyone knows and respects has a new and even better quality cigar. It's a cigar made for a king. It's a cigar made for a president. It's a cigar made for a dictator. But just like everyone else, they all just have to wait in line.

Ad Agency: Dunn&Co., Tampa, FL, USA | www.dunn-co.com   Client: Tourism Corporation Bonaire   Title: Climber

Art Directors: Alexandra Nieto   Creative Director: Troy Dunn

ASSIGNMENT

Bonaire is considered one of the top SCUBA diving locations in the world. The 112 square mile Caribbean island is home to 86 dive sites, surrounded by a reef teeming with life. However, Bonaire has more to offer tourists than just underwater wonders. With this in mind, Bonaire's tourism office asked us to develop travel agency posters that would promote the island's land-based activities.

APPROACH

We felt it was important to leverage Bonaire's solid reputation as "The Diver's Paradise" while delivering the land-activity message. This is what readers had come to expect from Bonaire. Also, we knew that it was vital to craft work that would stand out among the cookie-cutter "tropical" posters that typically plaster the walls of a travel agency. We figured travel posters were usually scanned quickly and therefore we needed something that would catch the reader off-guard enough that they would hesitate before moving on to the next poster. We wanted to suck them in by crafting work that was slightly off-center, requiring a double take.

THE BIG IDEA

Rather than the expectably beautiful, staged shot of someone partaking in a non-diving activity such as biking, kayaking or hiking on Bonaire, we chose a few above-water activities and put them in a setting that people don't normally associate them with — underwater. The two executions showcased here — Climber and Biker — work by grabbing the viewer's attention in their unconventional combination of above-water and under-water imagery. The message is delivered through a clever, simple visual, and aided by the tagline "As much to do above water as there is below it."

RESULTS

While we had no way to track the direct impact of the posters on travelers' decisions to visit Bonaire, the client was exceptionally pleased with this innovative, creative approach of combining above and below water imagery and feedback from travel agencies has been very positive.

Bonaire. As much to do above water as there is below it.

BONAIRE
Once a Visitor Always a Friend

Bonaire. As much to do above water as there is below it.

BONAIRE
Once a Visitor Always a Friend

Ad Agency: Lewis Communications, Birmingham, AL, USA | www.lewiscommunications.com   **Client:** Aquila Safari Game Reserve   **Title:** Aquila Ad Campaign
Art Director: Spencer Till   **Copywriters:** Stephen Curry, Spencer Till   **Executive Creative Director:** Spencer Till
Photographers: Jeff Williams, Stuuert   **Print Producers:** Benjamin Fine, Leigh Ann Motley

Most travelers who go on safari in South Africa tend to lean towards the giant game parks such as Kruger National Park, on the country's eastern side. There are comparatively fewer safari experiences on the Western Cape, where tourism more frequently draws visitors to Cape Town and the Winelands. We wanted to convey a message to Cape Town visitors that Aquila offers a luxurious safari experience, conveniently nearby, together with comfortable accommodations and top-notch food. Our goal was to artfully combine the sense of luxury with the stunning natural scenery, to give Western Cape visitors an accurate picture of the fantastic safari experience that lies only a couple of hours away.

Ad Agency: Michael Schwab Studio, San Anselmo, CA, USA | www.michaelschwab.com   **Client:** Amtrak   **Title:** Amtrak 'Sunset Limited'

Art Directors: trace-E ann Nenna   **Creative Director:** Woody Kay   **Designer:** Michael Schwab   **Illustrator:** Michael Schwab

ASSIGNMENT

Back in 2003, Arnold Worldwide inherited a well-known brand in Amtrak. But its 98% name awareness was not nearly matched by the public's travel interest — only 6% of adults rode Amtrak per year. The challenge was to increase ridership and revenue, but the train simply couldn't compete with the speed of air travel or the affordability and flexibility of hopping in the car.

APPROACH

So Arnold focused on the one area where Amtrak had a huge advantage: the experience.

THE BIG IDEA

A series of posters that capture the Romance of the Rail. Arnold commissioned graphic artist Michael Schwab to tap into the aesthetic of posters from the glory days of travel. Before there were middle seats or combination gas-station-fast-food restaurants. They remind people that, for all our "modern conveniences," one of the most important reasons to travel is for the travel itself. Or, as Amtrak's new tagline sums it up: Enjoy The Journey.

RESULTS

Arnold Worldwide and Amtrak have continued to commission posters in the growing Michael Schwab series that has been part of an extremely successful advertising program. In the first quarter of fiscal year 2010, Amtrak recorded its biggest ridership numbers ever. If the trend continues, Amtrak will beat its yearly record from 2008 (which beat its 2007 record, which beat its 2005 record, which beat its 2004 record).

SUNSET LIMITED

LOS ANGELES to NEW ORLEANS

AMTRAK

Ad Agency: BCF, Virginia Beach, VA, USA | www.boomyourbrand.com　　　　　　　　　　　　　　**Client:** Virginia Beach Tourism　　　　　　　　　　　　　**Title:** Live For Ads

Account Directors: Greg Ward, Eric Lonning　　　**Agency Producer:** Mandy Lui　　**Art Directors:** Joe Schnellmann, Erika Gonzalez　　**Copywriters:** Ginny Petty, Kevin McCarthy

Creative Director: Keith Ireland　　　　　　　　　　　　　　　　**Designer:** Todd Aftel　　　　　　　　　**Project Manager:** Laura Bolt

BCF created this campaign as an evolution of the Virginia Beach Convention and Visitor Board's existing "Live the Life" brand. The campaign gives a first-person, immersive look into Living the Life in Virginia Beach and allows us all to see ourselves experiencing the beach life along the shores of Virginia Beach.

The fully integrated campaign consists of traditional print, outdoor, online banner advertising and a fully immersive microsite, livethelife.com. With more than 40 films and interactive content, visitors to the site are welcomed to an unmatched landscape of everything that is the beach vibe.

An interesting fact about the entire Live For campaign is that it was done entirely in-house. From concept to campaign launch: writing, art direction, still photography, filming, editing, retouching, compositing, color correction, programming, animating, you name it — we did it. I guess you could say we Live For great work.

Ad Agency: Steven Taylor & Associates, London, UK   **Client:** Edmiston & Company   **Title:** Edmiston Charter   **Art Director:** Steven Taylor

ASSIGNMENT

This advertising campaign was designed to attract potential clients to charter a luxury yacht. As a luxury yacht of this size rarely charters for less than a six figure fee per week, the media selection and message were critically important. Edmiston is a broker of the world's finest yachts for sale or charter. As such there was an important balance to be struck between the message, the object (the yacht) and promoting the subliminal element of Edmiston's corporate identity — the color red.

THE CHALLENGE

The difficulty when creating advertising for items of such a limited appeal is to convey the perfect trigger to the very tiny minority who will understand the message. What is fantasy to most of us, is reality to the few. Communicating aspirational thoughts is actually about creating inspirational ideas.

THE CREATIVE PROCESS

The photographs in the campaign were shot by Steven Taylor & Associates for the individual yacht's brochures. When the decision was made to create a generic advertising campaign for Edmiston, we created themes/headlines to marry picture to headline balancing the fact that the message and photograph were equally important. Without both elements, either one would not communicate the message. The campaign also had to work in the context of the other marketing tools that support the brand including the charter brochure that is the response to enquiries.

RESULTS

The campaign was designed to be an extension of the entire integrated marketing effort. Sales and marketing are as one and Edmiston is accepted as one of the leading company's in its field. In a market where many competing companies charter the same yachts, this campaign reinforced the Edmiston reputation as the best name from which to charter a yacht.

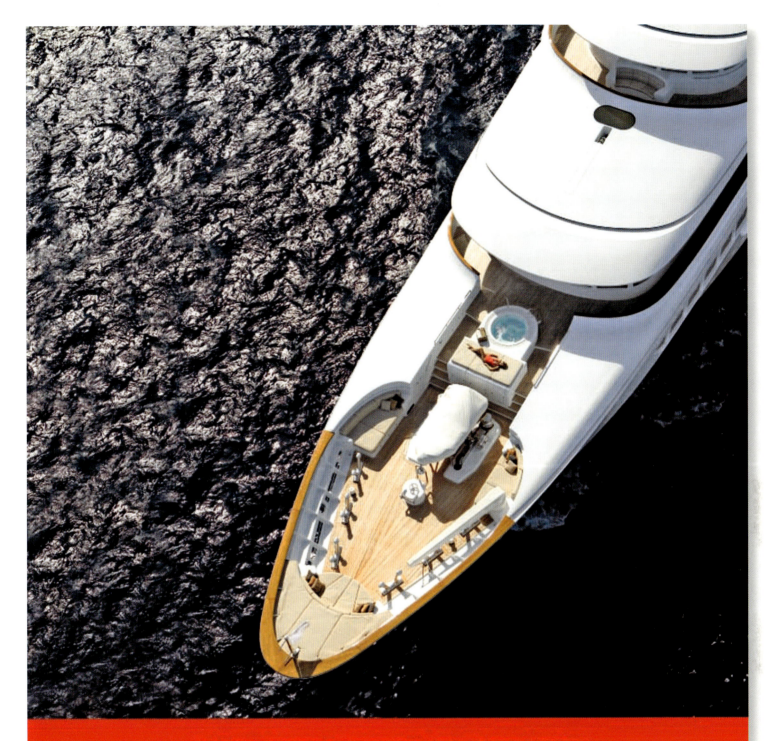

Ad Agency: MacLaren McCann Toronto, Canada | www.maclaren.com   **Client:** Prince Edward Sailing Charters   **Title:** Prince Edward Sailing Campaign

Art Directors: Scott Couture, Gary Lennox   **Executive Creative Director:** Sean Davison

The creative idea for this campaign can be summed up simply: the population of Prince Edward County on any given summer weekend is approximately 45 billion people. The population of a sailboat on any given summer is approximately six. So we decided to position Prince Edward Sailing Charters as a vacation within a vacation. It's a lulling respite from the 'gotta-do-everything' approach most urbanistas take to the holiday, with a whiff of the pirate in every excursion. Of course, the production budget for something like this can be described as miniscule to start, falling to zero as time goes on. Therefore, the art director was also the photographer and the writer strong armed the agency studio into printing posters for nothing. Media, thankfully, was simple. Wild postings, grocery store bulletin boards, cooperative restaurants and artfully scattered printouts gave a surprising amount of punch.

Yo ho ho and a bottle of Shiraz

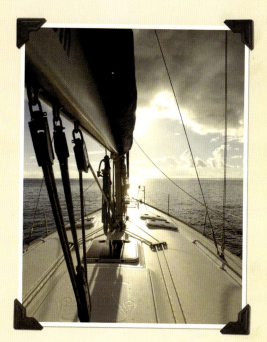

Beats shopping Main Street for more dreamcatchers and fudge.

Ad Agency: Martin|Williams, Minneapolis, USA | www.martinwilliams.com   **Client:** Marvin Integrity   **Title:** Carl & Stu Website

Agency Producers: Rick Fuller, Stan Prinsen   **Art Director:** Toby Balai   **Chief Creative Officer:** Tom Moudry

Copywriter: Adam Ridgeway   **Creative Directors:** Randy Tatum, Steve Casey   **Director:** Josh Thacker

Minnesota-based Integrity Windows and Doors offered products superior to their competitors. The only problem: builders didn't know they existed. Martin|Williams was charged with attracting trade professionals to educate them about the highly technical benefits of Integrity — without putting anyone to sleep.

Armed with knowledge that builders enjoyed learning through entertainment-based programs like Mythbusters and Dirty Jobs, we developed a fun-loving, jumpsuit-clad duo named Carl and Stu to perform pseudo product tests and demonstrate the virtues of Integrity products in a series of online videos. After two years of success, it launched them into near celebrity status and it was time for Carl & Stu to have their own show.

The Carl & Stu Show website features a Merv Griffin-esque set built from materials you'd only find in a construction warehouse. The duo's inexperience with Do It Yourself broadcast production leads to hilarity as Carl and Stu attempt to cover "serious topics" in the world of windows and doors. With an interactive experience that tapped into builders' thirst for edutainment, the Carl & Stu show found surprising success in an industry that seemed to be set in its ways.

Ad Agency: bpg, Los Angeles, USA | www.bigpicturegroup.net   **Client:** MovieTickets.com   **Title:** The Train   **Creative Director:** Steph Sebbag

The client's service offers a simple value proposition: the piece of mind of knowing your movie is not sold out. Using the dramatic metaphor of a man missing a train, we show the emotional consequences of missing your next movie. The spot ran on 13,000 theaters.

Don't miss another show.

Next time, buy your tickets in advance.

movietickets.com™

www.movietickets.com   mobile.movietickets.com   1-877-789-MOVIE

Ad Agency: BBDO West, San Francisco, USA | www.bbdo.com   **Client:** San Francisco Zoo   **Title:** The Zoo Misses You

Art Director: Marcus Brown   **Copywriters:** Neil Levy, Alex Grinton   **Creative Director:** Neil Levy   **Executive Creative Directors:** Jim Lesser, Jon Soto

To help increase zoo attendance, this thought was brought to life with a multi-dimensional advertising campaign featuring humans personified as animals doing their best to try to get people to be friends with them in a less-than-interested world.

AD AGENCIES

22squared	184
Apple	86
Bailey Lauerman	112
BBDO West	78, 232
BCF	52, 74, 220
Bill Santry Design	192
bpg	62, 76, 228
BradfordLawton, LLC	98
The Brandon Agency	42
Brian Kuhlmann Studio	138
Bussolati Associates	202
Butler, Shine, Stern & Partners	106
bvk	60, 170, 174, 182
Clarity Coverdale Fury	66, 178
Colle + McVoy	70, 118
Concussion LLP	190
Cramer Krasselt	40, 116
Davidson Branding	196
DeVito/Verdi	58, 188, 212
Duncan/Channon	194
Dunn&Co.	214
Erickson Productions, Inc.	204
Euro RSCG Chicago	186
Factory Design Labs	200
Goodby, Silverstein & Partners	36, 82, 88, 92, 110, 162, 206
Heller Communication Design	156
JWT Chile	140
JWT Sydney	120
Karo Group Inc.	136
KNARF	64, 72, 90
Laughlin Constable	172, 176
Lewis Communications	38, 166, 216
Lindsay, Stone & Briggs	96, 154
Lloyd & Company Advertising, Inc.	100
MacLaren McCann Calgary	48, 54, 132, 142
MacLaren McCann Toronto	224
Mangos	208
The Martin Agency	122, 126, 128, 210, 230
Martin | Williams	164, 226
MD70	104
Michael Schwab Studio	218
Muller Bressler Brown	94
O'Leary & Partners	44, 152
Ogilvy & Mather	56
Publicis Dallas	144, 146
Pyper Paul + Kenney	46, 68, 114, 168, 180
The Refinery	80, 108
Shine	50
Steven Taylor & Associates	222
STIR	34
STUDIO INTERNATIONAL	124
TAXI CANADA INC	84, 148, 150, 160
TBWA\Barcelona	102
TBWA\Brussels	134
TBWA\PHS Helsinki	158, 198
TBWA\RAAD	130

CLIENTS

3 Bar and Grill	192
AAA Mid-Atlantic	152
Adidas	102
Ambiance by Levis Paints (Akzo Nobel)	134
Amtrak	218
Apple	86
Appleton Estates Rum	58
Aquila Safari Game Reserve	216
ASPCA	168
Best Golf Cars	42
Boy Scouts of America	164
Bussolati	202
Can-Am Spyder Roadster	40
Cannondale Bicycle Corporation	208
City of Milwaukee County Health Department	170, 174
Coca-Cola/Hopenhagen	56
Comcast	82
Comcast Sports Network	78
CommuniTea Café	54
ConAgra Foods	112
Creative Edge Parties	156
Discovery Channel	74
E.P. Carillo Cigars	212
Edmiston & Company	222
Ellington Fans	138
Erickson Stock	204
Fox Broadcasting Company	80
The Fridge	130
Gold's Gym	160
Habitat for Humanity	166
Hardly Strictly Bluegrass	92
Hazco Demolition	150
Healtheries	50
Hewlett Packard	88, 162
History	62
Hyundai	36
Instrumentarium	198
Jailhouse Fire	68, 114
Jazz at Five	96
Jil Sander	100
JFK Presidential Library & Museum	122, 126, 128, 230
Kansas International Film Festival	94
Legal Sea Foods	188
Lewis Energy	98
Marvin Integrity	226
Massimo Zanetti Beverage	52
Metropolitan Ministries	180
Milwaukee County DA	60
Minnesota State Lottery	70
Mothers Against Drunk Driving	178
Mothers Polishes	44
MovieTickets.com	228
Mr. Nils	104
Museum Documentation Centre	124
NASCAR	210
NBA	206
Nestle	120
Nestle Purina	118
Newcity	186
Otterbottle Inc.	136
Pak-N-Stor	148
Partnership For A Drug-Free America	184
PC Medic	84
Prince Edward Sailing Charters	224
The Psychic Gallery	154
Quaker	110
Randell's Drycleaning	142
Recordland	132
Red Cross	172
Red Gold	66
Revo	200
Ronald McDonald House	176
San Francisco Zoo	232
Sanita Clogs, Inc	194
School of Visual Arts	64, 72, 90
Scrabble	140
Screen Gems	108
Secrets Shhh	196
Shooting Star Casino	190
Smoothe Laser Clinics	48
Sorel	106
Spice Islands	116
Syfy	76
Terminix	144, 146
Tiffin Motorhomes	38
Tires Plus	46
Tourism Corporation Bonaire	214
United Way	182
Urban Motorworx	34
Virginia Beach Tourism	220
Young Director Award by CFP-E/Shots	158

ART DIRECTORS

Ameye, Alex	134
Ammermann, Carrie	106
Anselmo, Frank	64, 72, 90
Atienza, Jayson	72
Balai, Toby	164, 226
Bickell, Jason	166
Birch, Jeff	80
Black, Dustin	70
Brown, Marcus	232
Cheeseman, Len	50
Christensen, Paul	152
Copiz, Stefan	82
Couture, Scott	224
Curtis, Jelani	64
Day, Ben	180
Dimmer, Matt	186
Dunkerley, Sean	80, 108
Ecton, Josh	80
Evans, Jason	100
Gonzalez, Erika	220
Gonzalez, Zara	118
Gregoire, Kris	46, 68
Halpin, Ben	182
Heller, Cheryl	156
Holpfer, Shawn	40
Honkanen, Ossi	198
Hooker, Randall	210
Horne, Kelsey	84, 148, 150, 160
Ireland, Keith	52, 74
Johanning, Matt	34, 96, 154
Kenny, Tom	114
Kimber, Blair	120
Kirkman, Derek	184
Kohnke, Rich	170
Kupets, Masha	62
Lavola, Minna	158
Lecaros, Matías	140
Lee, GiHo	182
Lennox, Gary	224
Leon, Jon	42
Lloyd, Douglas	100
Logan, Cris	110
Lovely, Mark	54, 132
Ljubicic, Boris	124
Madcharo, Karl	178
Markes, Dave	112
Massis, Andre	162
Meadus, Mike	54, 132, 142
Meis, Ryan	88
Melvin, Sherrod	58
Menna, Zack	58, 188
Miller, Derek	208
Mitchell, Sean	48
Nauta, Chad	176
Nenna, trace-E ann	218
Nieto, Alexandra	214
Peaslee, Cheryl	174
Reynolds, George	138
Rho, Richard	76
Riney, Aaron	68, 168
Rins, Jordi	102
Root, Jim	116
Ryan, Matt	206
Sack, Ron	112
Santos, Manny	212
Santry, Bill	192
Santucci, Natalie	142
Scalise, Mike	60, 174
Schnellmann, Joe	220
Shade, Claude	92
Shymko, Scott	136
Spiegler, Eric	44
Steinseifer, Brian	40
Tarver, Melody	138
Taylor, Dustin	144, 146
Taylor, Steven	222
Till, Derek	118
Till, Spencer	38, 166, 216
Tisser, Jason	186
Toland, Chris	36
Torvinen, Mikko	198
Valle, Michael	80
Vojvodich, Michael	172
Walsh, Justin	56
Wang, William	64
Weinblatt, Lauren	78
Wilde, Richard	64
Williams, Brian	122, 126, 128, 230
Yi, Jeseok	64
Young, Amy	94

CREATIVE DIRECTORS

Alexander, Joe 122, 126, 128, 230
Amsler, Marty 112
Apple Graphic Design 86
Atienza, Jayson 72
Barrett, Jamie 82, 110, 206
Burton, Trent 84, 146, 150, 160
Bussolati, Monica 202
Casey, Steve 226
Copithorne, Phil 136
Copiz, Stefan 82, 206
Coverdale, Jac 178
Curry, Stephen 38, 166
de Menna, Joanne 208
DeVito, Sal 188, 212
Dunn, Troy 214
Elisco-Lemme, Anne 194

Emmett, Brad 58
Fazende, Michael 116
Ford, Chris 82
Goodby, Jeff 36, 92
Grimes, Steve 144, 146
Gunderson, Brian 88
Hanneken, David 172, 176
Hochberg, Brad 80, 108
Holmstrom, Johan 104
Husband, Eric 118
Ireland, Keith 52, 74, 220
Jacobs, Chris 116
Kay, Woody 218
Keepper, Dave 70
Kohnke, Rich 170
Kresse, Bill 34

Law, Lucien 50
Lecaros, Matías 140
Levy, Neil 232
Macken, Jan 134
McGinness, Will 110, 162
Meadus, Mike 48, 54, 132, 142
Melle, Julia 144, 146
Mueller, Gary 60, 170, 174 182
Neely, Shan 94
Park, John 88
Rosati, Sergio 140
Sales, Miquel 102
Santry, Bill 192
Sebbag, Steph 62, 76, 228
Simpson, Steve 88
Sorah, Cliff 210

Stapleton, John 184
Stone, Todd 40
Tatum, Randy 226
Torvinen, Mikko 198
Tresidder, Jeff 164
Tricklebank, Ben 230
Voehringer, Pete 144, 146
Waldman, Adam 108
Weiss, Ari 206
Wilde, Richard 64, 72, 90
Wills, Josh 200
Winchester, Bill 96
Yi, Jeseok 64

EXECUTIVE CREATIVE DIRECTORS

Anselmo, Frank 64, 72, 90
Butler, John 106
Caguin, Mike 70, 118
Coates, Tom 106
Coverdale, Jac 66
Davison, Sean 224
DeVito, Sal 58

Earley, Joe 80
Farfan, Leo 140
Fraser, Andrew 120
Fredrick, Jim 108
Gast, Bradley 208
Godici, Tom 56
Hills, Jon 230

Jacobs, Chris 40
Jamison, Tiffany 106
Kenney, Tom 46, 68, 114, 168, 180
Ketchum, Greg 56
Lesser, Jim 78, 232
McQuaide, Deidre 44, 152
Morrissey, Tom 80

Rathbone, Shon 144, 146
Shine, Mike 106
Soto, Jon 78, 232
Spiegler, Eric 44, 152
Till, Spencer 38, 166, 216
Vamosy, Michael 80
Whittier, Steve 200

ASSOCIATE CREATIVE DIRECTORS

Burns, Roy 166
Crawford, Joey 180
Gerstner, Greg 56

Lam, John 120
Moll, Justin 208
Pittman, Nicolle 54, 142

Schillig, Michael 46, 68, 114, 168
Shalles, Scott 34
Smolover, Charles 208

ACCOUNT DIRECTORS

Anteroinena, Eija 198
Bailey, Beth 38
Bennett, Brian 34
Bird, Carrie 122, 126, 128, 230
Blakely, Leigh 136
Bull, Jarrod 230

Burns, Roy 166
Crowell, Lindsay 98
Diamond, Tony 98
Ellis, Gord 160
Garcia, Garrett 46
Hardekopf, Sarah 38

Holman, Val 38
Jamin, Jenny 80, 108
Lonning, Eric 74, 220
Norris, Larry 166
Rope, Kam 200
Schindele, Scott 52

Strickland, Miriam 166
Vahsholtz, Jesse 46, 168
Ward, Greg 220
Wetmore, Ginny 84, 150

DESIGNERS

Aftel, Todd 220
Balerite, Kris 130
Bussolati, Monica 202
Cicala, Stephen 50
Cisneros, Boris 80

Holmewood, Emile 50
Krinsky, Nicki 204
Lawton, Bradford 98
Ljubicic, Boris 124
Mardisalu, Margit 158

Meadus, Mike 132
Meis, Ryan 88
Neuman, Sara 34
Plavec, Breda 130
Schwab, Michael 218

Seybert, Sarah 156
Tamminen, Sanna 158
van der Westhuyzen, Andrew 120
Zapata, Josh 98

ILLUSTRATORS

Bannecker, Andrew 56
Berstel, Boris 140

Fake Graphics 158
Replicate Designs 150

Schwab, Michael 218
Vallisto, Tommi 198

PHOTOGRAPHERS

Almas, Erik 106
Bengstsson, Morten 194
Chapman, Jonathan 118
Clark, William 178
Clemmons, Justin 144
Collura, Nick 170
Day, Ben 180
Erickson, Jim 204
Ervin, Bob 112

Fallis, Noah 48
Furman, Michael 208
Gastello, Cristián 140
Gyssler, Glen 60
Harben, Scott 146
Hietala, Jere 158
Kleveter, Mike 112
Lacoursiere, Justen 54, 132, 142, 160
Lysne, Colby 94

McDonald, Jim 174
Perron, Jean 136
Riney, Aaron 114
Salzer, Jeff 40, 116, 176
Schultz, Richard 200
Scott, Zachary 88
Serrano, Ramon 102
Shade, Claude 92, 162
Silk, Matt 42

Smith, Brian Bowen 80
Stallaert, Kurt 134
Stang, Jason 148, 150
Stuuert 216
Umland, Steve 66
Williams, Jeff 38, 166, 216
Wonnacott, Martin 58

COPYWRITERS

Alger, Wade 122, 126, 128, 230	Curry, Stephen 166, 216	Lecaros, Matias 140	Reynolds, Craig 136
Anselmo, Frank 72	Curtis, Jelani 64	Lehto, Aimee 106	Ridgeway, Adam 164, 226
Armour, Simon 120	DerHovsepian, Sandy 116	Levy, Neil 232	Ritchie, Brian 118
Asik, Nick 84, 148, 150, 160	Donoho, Tommy 94	Makinen, Tommy 198	Rosene, James 42
Atienza, Jayson 72	Elliott, Jim 36	Mannila, Erkko 198	Rowell, Rainbow 112
Atkinson, Michael 178	Emmett, Brad 58	McCarthy, Kevin 52, 74, 220	Schillig, Michael 46, 68, 114, 168
Barrett, Jamie 110	Ford, Chris 82	McNelis, Matt 152	Schmidt, Lee 96, 154
Barti, Michael 78	Gelber, Manor 58	Mitchell, Sean 48, 132	Schutte, Eric 212
Beckman, Andrew 144, 146	Grinton, Alex 232	Morin, Wilfrid 134	Shalles, Scott 34
Billows, Mark 210	Haapalehto, Markku 158	Mueller, Gary 182	Spratt, Aaron 192
Botfeld, Kevin 184	Hanneken, David 172	Neerland, John 70	Till, Spencer 38, 166, 216
Brady, Mike 166	Hoercher, Ryan 82	Nguyen, Duc 90	Toivonen, Antti 198
Calzina, Albert 102	Holicek, Mike 60, 170, 174	Olsson, Mira 158	Wang, William 64
Channon, Parker 194	Jacobs, Chris 40	Park, John 88	Weiss, Ari 206
Charney, Paul 82	King, Mike 200	Petty, Ginny 220	
Chin, Brian 40	Kline, Regan 186	Pihl, Bonnie 188	
Copithorne, Phil 136	Kramer, Jordan 162	Pittman, Nicolle 54, 132, 142	

DIGITAL ARTISTS / MULTIMEDIA

Ferrise, Gina 172, 176	Metcalf, Chris 172, 176	Safwenberg, Petter 230	Wise, Chris 230
Liobrera, Mark 230	Moe, Jennifer 194	Steenstry, Brian 34	Young, Justin 230
McDonald, Jim 170, 174	Rodrigues, Saulo 230	Trelles, Oscar 230	

AGENCY PRODUCERS

Lui, Mandy 74, 220	Prinsen, Stan 226	Fretwell, Darbi 230	Hubert, Steven 230
Fuller, Rick 226	Bobinski, Brian 52	Kwee, Norma 230	Roderer, Jaime 146

PRINT PRODUCERS

Barrabee, Suzee 206	Fuller, Rachel 56	Nunnelee, Lauren 208	Walters, Marsha 84, 150, 160
Cooper, Diane 80	Hick, Cindy 230	Piscatelli, Michael 56	
Fine, Benjamin 38, 166, 216	Knaeps, Carol 44	Schoenherr, Jenny 122, 126, 128	
Fodor, Jacqueline 194	Motley, Leigh Ann 38, 166, 216	Theiss, Katy 144	

ADDITIONAL CONTRIBUTORS

Bolt, Laura/Project Manager 52, 74, 220	Ghassab, Hadoum/Account Manage 134	Mattsson, Karolina/Project Manager 198	Robie, Christine/Account Supervisor 134
Ebel, Blake/Chief Creative Officer 186	Gruneberg, Andrea/Design Director 130	Meng, Tham Khai/Chief Creative Officer 56	Teughels, Annick/Advertiser's Supervisor . 134
Fine, Benjamin/Photographer's Assistant	Hacjob/Artist 38	Morgan, Tammy/Project Manager 196	Thacker, Josh/Director 226
.... 38, 166	Hausrath, Stephen/Artist 200	Moudry, Tom/Chief Creative Officer ... 164, 226	Vaile, Jim/Editor 230
Gao, Shang/Editor 230	Magic Group Amsterdam/Marianne Gualtieri	Olivo, Jeff/Project Manager 208	Yanez, Andrew/Chief Creative Officer 190
	(TBWA\)/Illustrator Photo-Retouching 134	Parni, Kirsi/Project Manager 158, 198	

22squared www.22squared.com
401 East Jackson Street, Suite 3600
Tampa, FL 33602, United States
Tel 813 202 1227 | Fax 813 926 3093

Apple www.apple.com
1 Infinite Loop, MS 83-PPS
Cupertino, CA 95014, United States
Tel 408 974 5286

Bailey Lauerman
www.baileylauerman.com
1248 O Street, Suite 900
Lincoln, NE 68508, United States
Tel 402 479 0235

BBDO West San Francisco www.bbdo.com
555 Market Street, 17th Floor
San Francisco, CA 94105, United States
Tel 415 808 6212

BCF www.boomyourbrand.com
240 Business Park Drive
Virginia Beach, VA 23462, United States
Tel 757 497 4811

Bill Santry Design
www.billsantrydesign.com
2520 23rd Road North
Arlington, VA 22207, United States
Tel 703 528 2465

bpg www.bigpicturegroup.net
110 S Fairfax Avenue, Suite 355
Los Angeles, CA 90036, United States
Tel 323 954 9522

BradfordLawton, LLC
www.bradfordlawton.com
1020 Townsend Avenue
San Antonio, TX 78209, United States
Tel 210 832 0555 | Fax 210 832 0007

Brian Kuhlmann Studio
www.briankuhlmann.com
1932 South Halsted, Studio 101
Chicago, IL 60608, United States
Tel 312 794 5223

Bussolati Associates www.bussolati.com
1541 14th Street NW
Washington, DC 20005, United States
Tel 202 319 2222 | Fax 202 319 2223

Butler, Shine, Stern & Partners
www.bssp.com
20 Liberty Ship Way
Sausalito, CA 94965, United States
Tel 415 944 8279

bvk www.bvk.com
250 West Coventry Court, Suite 300
Milwaukee, WI 53217, United States
Tel 414 228 1990

Clarity Coverdale Fury
www.claritycoverdalefury.com
120 South 6th Street, Suite 1300
Minneapolis, MN 55402, United States
Tel 612 359 4337

Colle + McVoy
www.collemcvoy.com
400 First Avenue North, Suite 700
Minneapolis, MN 55401, United States
Tel 612 305 6169

Concussion LLP www.concussion.net
707 West Vickery Boulevard
Fort Worth, TX 76104, United States
Tel 817 336 6824

Cramer Krasselt www.c-k.com
246 East Chicago Street
Milwaukee, WI 53202, United States
Tel 414 227 3510

Davidson Branding
www.davidsonbranding.com
19 Amsterdam Street
Richmond, Victoria 3121, Australia
Tel + 61 3 9429 1288

Devito/Verdi www.devitoverdi.com
100 5th Avenue
New York, NY 10011, United States
Tel 212 431 4694 | Fax 212 431 4940

Duncan/Channon
www.duncanchannon.com
114 Sansome Street, 14th Floor
San FranciscoCA 94104
United States
Tel 415 306 9200

Dunn&Co. www.dunn-co.com
202 South 22nd Street, Ste. 202
Tampa, FL 33605, United States
Fax 813 273 8116

Erickson Productions, Inc.
www.ericksonproductions.com
2 Liberty Street
Petaluma, CA 94952, United States
Tel 707 789 0405

Euro RSCG Chicago
www.eurorscgchicago.com
36 East Grand Avenue
Chicago, IL 60611, United States
Tel 312 640 3240

Factory Design Labs
www.factorylabs.com
158 Fillmore Street
Denver, CO 80206, United States
Tel 720 224 9518

Goodby, Silverstein & Partners
www.goodbysilverstein.com
720 California Street
San Francisco, CA 94108, United States
Tel 415 955 5683

Heller Communication Design
www.hellercd.com
100 Jay Street, Apartment 12C
Brooklyn, NY 11201, United States
Tel 610 888 5580

JWT Chile www.jwt.com
Ricardo Lyon 1262, Santiago, Chile
Tel +56 (0)2 230 9000

JWT Sydney www.jwt.com.au
Level 14, 338 Pitt Street
Sydney, NSW 2000, Australia
Tel +61 2 9947 2222

Karo Group Inc. www.karo.com
1817 10th Avenue SW
Calgary, Alberta T3C 0K2, Canada
Tel +403 266 4094

KNARF www.knarfny.com
10 West 15th Street, #204
New York, NY 10011, United States
Tel 212 645 6277

Laughlin Constable www.laughlin.com
207 East Michigan Street
Milwaukee, WI 53202, United States
Tel 414 270 7221

Lewis Communications
www.lewiscommunications.com
600 Corporate Parkway, Suite 200
Birmingham AL, 35242, United States
Tel 205 980 0774

Lindsay, Stone & Briggs www.lsb.com
100 State Street, Madison WI, 53703
United States | Tel 608 251 7070

Lloyd & Company Advertising, Inc.
www.lloydandco.com
180 Varick Street, Suite 1018
New York, NY 10014, United States
Tel 212 414 3100 | Fax 212 414 3113

MacLaren McCann Calgary
www.maclaren.com
238 11th Avenue SE
Calgary, Alberta T2G 0X8, Canada
Tel 403 261 7155

MacLaren McCann Toronto
www.maclaren.com
10 Bay Street, 14th Floor
Toronto Ontario, M5J 2S3, Canada
Tel 416 594 6000

Mangos www.mangosinc.com
10 Great Valley Parkway
Malvern, PA 19355, United States
Tel 610 296 2555

Martin Williams
www.martinwilliams.com
60 South Sixth Street, Suite 2800
Minneapolis, MN 55402, United States
Tel 612 342 9689

MD70 www.md70.com
601 West 26th Street, Suite 835
New York, NY 10001, United States
Tel 212 242 6009

Michael Schwab Studio
www.michaelschwab.com
108 Tamalpais Avenue
San Anselmo, CA 94960, United States
Tel 415 257 5792

Muller Bressler Brown
www.mbbagency.com
4739 Belleview, Suite 100
Kansas City, MO 64112, United States
Tel 816 300 6303

O'Leary & Partners
www.olearyandpartners.com
5000 Birch Street, Suite 1000
Newport Beach, CA 92660, United States
Tel 949 833 8006 | Fax 949 833 9155

Ogilvy & Mather www.ogilvy.com
636 11th Avenue
New York, NY 10036, United States
Tel 212 237 7491

Publicis Dallas www.publicis-usa.com
7300 Lone Star Drive, Suite 200
Plano, TX 75024, United States
Tel 469 366 2305

Pyper Paul + Kenney www.pyperpaul.com
1102 North Florida Avenue
Tampa, FL 33602, United States
Tel 813 496 7000 | Fax 813 496 7002

Shine www.shinelimited.co.nz
18 Drake Street
Freemans Bay, Auckland 1010, New Zealand
Tel +64 9 373 4430

Steven Taylor & Associates
The Plaza, Unit 3.17, 535 Kings Road
London SW10 0SZ, United Kingdom
Tel +0044 20 73512345

STIR www.stirstuff.com
252 East Highland Avenue
Milwaukee, WI 53202, United States
Tel 414 278 0040 | Fax 414 278 0390

STUDIO INTERNATIONAL
www.studio-international.com
Buconjieva 43/III, Zagreb, HR-10 000 Croatia
(Local Name: Hrvatska)
Tel +385 1 37 40 404 | Fax +385 1 37 08 320

TAXI CANADA INC - Toronto www.taxi.ca
495 Wellington Street West, Suite 102
Ontario M5V 1E9, Canada
Tel 416 342 8294 | F 416 979 7626

TAXI CANADA INC - Calgary www.taxi.ca
805 Tenth Avenue Southwest, Suite 500,
Calgary, Alberta, Canada, T2R 0B4
Tel 403 269 8294 | Fax 403 269 7776

TBWA\Barcelona www.tbwa.es
Paseo de Gracia, 56, 2º Piso
08007 Barcelona, Spain
Tel +34 93 272 36 36

TBWA\Brussels www.tbwagroup.be
Kroonlaan 165 av. de la Couronne
B-1050 Brussels, Belgium
Tel +32 (0) 2 789 39 40

TBWA\PHS Helsinki www.tbwa.fi
Fredrikinkatu 42
00100 Helsinki, Finland
Tel +358(0)10 270 4100 | Fax +358(0)10 270 4800

TBWA\RAAD www.tbwaraad.com
Emaar Square, Building 1, Level 6
Dubai, United Arab Emirates
Tel +9714 4258888

The Brandon Agency
www.thebrandonagency.com
3023 Church Street
Myrtle Beach, SC 29577, United States
Tel 843 916 2033

The Martin Agency www.martinagency.com
One Shockoe Plaza
Richmond, VA 23219, United States
Tel 804 698 8750

The Refinery www.therefinerycreative.com
115 N. Hollywood Way
Burbank, CA 91505, United States
Tel 818 843 0004 | Fax 818 843 0029

Poster Annual 2011

Design Annual 2011

New Talent Annual 2010

100 Best Annual Reports 2010

Promotion Design 2

Brochures 6

Letterhead 7

Logo Design 7

Product Design 3

Masters of the 20th Century

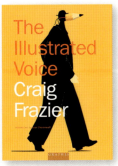
The Illustrated Voice

12 Japanese Masters

designing:
Chermayeff & Geismar

Exhibition:
The Work of Socio X

Design Journal Americas 001

"Had it not been for Ally&Gargano, Federal Express would probably not exist today."

Fred Smith, *FedEx Founder, Chairman, President & CEO*

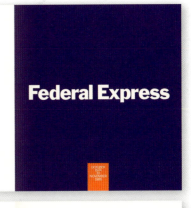